Social Marketing

Social Marketing has been co-published simultaneously
as *Journal of Nonprofit & Public Sector Marketing*, Volume 9,
Number 4 2001.

The *Journal of Nonprofit & Public Sector Marketing* Monographic "Separates"

Michael T. Ewing, PhD
Editor

Social Marketing

Social Marketing has been co-published simultaneously as Journal of Nonprofit & Public Sector Marketing, Volume 9, Number 4 2001.

Pre-publication
REVIEWS,
COMMENTARIES,
EVALUATIONS . . .

"IMPORTANT FOR MARKETING ACADEMICS AS WELL AS PRACTITIONERS. . . . Due to the fact that many of the ills of society are being blamed on the marketing discipline, it is imperative for us to understand marketing's contributions to society. This book provides insight into not only the phenomenal benefits that can accrue to society by means of the application of marketing principles and practices but also the potential pitfalls inherent in misapplications. The debate represented by this mixture of stimulating articles is extremely healthy for marketing as a discipline."

John B. Ford, PhD
Professor of Marketing and International Business
Old Dominion University
Norfolk, VA

Social Marketing

Michael T. Ewing, PhD
Editor

Social Marketing has been co-published simultaneously as *Journal of Nonprofit & Public Sector Marketing*, Volume 9, Number 4 2001.

BEST BUSINESS BOOKS

Best Business Books
An Imprint of
The Haworth Press, Inc.
New York • London • Oxford

Published by

Best Business Books®, 10 Alice Street, Binghamton, NY 13904-1580 USA

Best Business Books® is an imprint of The Haworth Press, Inc., 10 Alice Street, Binghamton, NY 13904-1580 USA.

Social Marketing has been co-published simultaneously as *Journal of Nonprofit & Public Sector Marketing*, Volume 9, Number 4 2001.

The development, preparation, and publication of this work has been undertaken with great care. However, the publisher, employees, editors, and agents of The Haworth Press and all imprints of The Haworth Press, Inc., including The Haworth Medical Press® and Pharmaceutical Products Press®, are not responsible for any errors contained herein or for consequences that may ensue from use of materials or information contained in this work. Opinions expressed by the author(s) are not necessarily those of The Haworth Press, Inc.

Cover design by Thomas J. Mayshock Jr.

Library of Congress Cataloging-in-Publication Data

Social marketing / Michael T. Ewing, editor.
    p. cm.
   "Social marketing has been co-published simultaneously as Journal of nonprofit & public sector marketing, volume 9, number 4, 2001."
   Includes bibliographical references and index.
   ISBN 0-7890-1716-4 (hc) - ISBN 0-7890-1717-2 (pbk)
   1. Social marketing. I. Ewing, Michael T.
HF5414 .S63 2002
658.8-dc21
                                                2002002632

Indexing, Abstracting & Website/Internet Coverage

This section provides you with a list of major indexing & abstracting services. That is to say, each service began covering this periodical during the year noted in the right column. Most Websites which are listed below have indicated that they will either post, disseminate, compile, archive, cite or alert their own Website users with research-based content from this work. (This list is as current as the copyright date of this publication.)

Abstracting, Website/Indexing Coverage . . . . Year When Coverage Began

- **BUBL Information Service, an Internet-based Information Service for the UK higher education community <URL:http://bubl.ac.uk/>** 1995

- **Business Source Elite (EBSCO)** 2001

- **Business Source Premier (EBSCO)** 2001

- **CNPIEC Reference Guide: Chinese National Directory of Foreign Periodicals** 1995

- **Contents of this publication are indexed and abstracted in the ABI/INFORM database, available on ProQuest Information & Learning <www.proquest.com>** 2002

- **ELMAR (Current Table of Contents Services), American Marketing Assn <http://www.ama.org/academic/elmar/>** 2001

- **FINDEX <www.publist.com>** 1999

- **Human Resources Abstracts (HRA)** 1993

- **IBZ International Bibliography of Periodical Literature <www.saur.de>** 1996

(continued)

Special Bibliographic Notes related to special journal issues (separates) and indexing/abstracting:

- indexing/abstracting services in this list will also cover material in any "separate" that is co-published simultaneously with Haworth's special thematic journal issue or DocuSerial. Indexing/abstracting usually covers material at the article/chapter level.
- monographic co-editions are intended for either non-subscribers or libraries which intend to purchase a second copy for their circulating collections.
- monographic co-editions are reported to all jobbers/wholesalers/approval plans. The source journal is listed as the "series" to assist the prevention of duplicate purchasing in the same manner utilized for books-in-series.
- to facilitate user/access services all indexing/abstracting services are encouraged to utilize the co-indexing entry note indicated at the bottom of the first page of each article/chapter/contribution.
- this is intended to assist a library user of any reference tool (whether print, electronic, online, or CD-ROM) to locate the monographic version if the library has purchased this version but not a subscription to the source journal.
- individual articles/chapters in any Haworth publication are also available through the Haworth Document Delivery Service (HDDS).

Social Marketing

CONTENTS

ABOUT THE EDITOR

Michael T. Ewing, PhD, is a professor of marketing at Monash University in Melbourne, Australia. Before entering academia, he was marketing research manager for Ford Motor Company in South Africa. He has taught in Australia, China, Hong Kong, Singapore, Malaysia, the Czech Republic, South Africa and England. His research focuses primarily on measuring marketing communications effects (often within a cross-cultural and/or nonprofit environment). He has published over 60 articles in refereed journals. Amongst others, his work has appeared in the *Journal of the Academy of Marketing Science*, the *Journal of Advertising Research*, the *Journal of Business Research*, the *International Journal of Advertising*, *Business Horizons* and *Industrial Marketing Management*. Dr. Ewing serves on the editorial boards of the *Journal of Advertising Research*, the *International Journal of Advertising*, the *Journal of Nonprofit & Public Sector Marketing* and the *Service Industries Journal*. He has 6 book chapters and over 70 refereed conference papers to his credit and has won numerous awards and citations for his research.

For more information or to order
the **Journal of Nonprofit & Public Sector Marketing,**
visit http://www.haworthpressinc.com/store/product.asp?sku=J054

- or call (800) HAWORTH (in US and Canada) or
  (607) 722-5857 (outside US and Canada)

- or fax (800) 895-0582 (in US and Canada) or
  (607) 771-0012 (outside US and Canada)

For a list of related links,
visit http://www.haworthpressinc.com/store/product.asp?sku=J054

Urge your library to subscribe today!
With your library's print subscription,
the electronic edition of the journal can
be made available campus-wide to all
of the library's users!

Preface

SOCIAL AND CAUSE-RELATED MARKETING:
THE GROWTH OF A DISCIPLINE?

Marketing has certainly come a long way in the past 30 years. It was Kotler and Levy (1969) who famously posited the notion that marketing could apply equally well to organizations lacking the profit motive, and just two years later, Kotler and Zaltman (1971), who explicitly included in marketing's remit the marketing of ideas. Defining it as *"the design, implementation and control of programmes calculated to influence the acceptability of social ideas and involving considerations of product planning, pricing, communication, distribution and marketing research,"* the authors studiously differentiated marketing from "education" or the "facilitation of a change of attitudes or values." Social marketing, in their view differed because its goal, just as in the commercial sector, should always be a change in "consumer" behaviour.

By the mid-1970s a consensus had emerged from the marketing literature that it was indeed perfectly legitimate to seek to extend marketing's influence to the nonprofit arena, and over the intervening years, there has been a slow but steady growth in awareness of this in both academic and practitioner circles. Charity fundraisers, for example, have long been making use of marketing tools and techniques. Indeed, fundraisers from the best-performing charities are now agency-trained and aware that to compete they must be "market oriented" and offer a very real service to their clients. Thus, in their dealings with the corporate sector, charities are increasingly seeking to work in partnership with their sponsors, offering a package of tangible and intangible benefits in exchange for monetary support, staff time or gifts in kind. Mar-

[Haworth co-indexing entry note]: "Preface." Sargeant, Adrian. Co-published simultaneously in *Journal of Nonprofit & Public Sector Marketing* (Best Business Books, an imprint of The Haworth Press, Inc.) Vol. 9, No. 4, 2001, pp. xiii-xv; and: *Social Marketing* (ed: Michael T. Ewing) Best Business Books, an imprint of The Haworth Press, Inc., 2001, pp. xi-xiii. Single or multiple copies of this article are available for a fee from The Haworth Document Delivery Service [1-800-HAWORTH, 9:00 a.m. - 5:00 p.m. (EST). E-mail address: getinfo@haworthpressinc.com].

keting has a clear role to play in facilitating this exchange, driven as it is by a fundamental understanding of what potential partners to such an exchange might be looking for in return for their support.

It is also increasingly recognized that marketing has a role to play at the societal level in stimulating additional support of the voluntary sector. In the U.K., the government's new Giving Campaign is already focussing on using marketing tools and techniques to persuade more Organizations to support charity and to encourage a greater proportion of the general public to give. These initiatives coupled with incentives such as the most radical reform of charity taxation in over 50 years and the facilitation of giving through the simplification of schemes such as Gift Aid and Payroll giving, combine to make this one of the most significant social marketing campaigns ever to be conducted.

Yet, despite the utility of marketing at both conceptual and functional levels, a number of objections continue to be raised. The road to acceptance of marketing in the nonprofit and social arenas has been far from easy. Marketing has often been accused of being invasive, immoral, lowering the quality of otherwise worthwhile work, and perhaps more subtly, creating conflict within some institutions between customer satisfaction and the achievement of the overall mission. This is often the case in arts organizations, for example, where marketing is frequently accused of compelling organizations to focus primarily on "popular" forms of art. It is perhaps in recognition of this that when asked to define marketing, the Artistic Director of a large nonprofit theatre once described it as "reprehensible!" Whilst having the merit of being somewhat shorter than many other definitions the author has encountered, this neglects the notion that as Kotler and Levy famously posited, marketing is about sensitively serving the needs of society and therefore about the achievement of some degree of balance.

In general, however, marketing has gained acceptance amongst the practitioner community, and as long ago as 1991, the consortium of Arts Council and Regional Arts Association Officers went on record as stating that marketing should be viewed as essential to increasing the perceived value of the arts in society. In the social sphere, marketing has also successfully touched our lives, warning us of the dangers of smoking, alcoholism and drug abuse and ensuring that the most vulnerable groups within society receive the support and understanding they deserve.

Of course, marketing expenditures in the realm of nonprofit and social marketing are often not great and pale into insignificance alongside the marketing spending of the major Organizations. Yet, despite this, it is important to recognize that the nonprofit sector in most societies, although typically contributing only around 5% to GDP, punches well above its weight in terms of its social and moral significance. Nonprofit marketing, in whatever guise, often attracts a disproportionate amount of attention and interest.

It is therefore somewhat surprising that there has not been rather more academic interest in the topic since nonprofit marketing was first mooted as an avenue for research in the early 1970s. To this day there are few marketing academics actively focussed on nonprofit research, and whilst a handful of others will from time to time dabble in the field, there has yet to be much real interest in the topic around much of the Western World. It remains possible to count on the fingers of one hand the number of nonprofit marketing courses offered in the US and indeed the number of Professors of Nonprofit Marketing around the world. Publication in the top journals remains problematic, as these have historically been heavily focussed on business concerns and access to research funds is limited as national research councils focus heavily on what they perceive as more worthy for-profit areas of management research.

Yet, the picture is not all gloomy. The volume of high-quality nonprofit research continues to increase each year. The number of sector journals has doubled in ten years and for the first time, two US institutions will be offering nonprofit marketing positions later this year. There are also special issues such as this, which will play an increasingly important role in stimulating wider research into nonprofit and social marketing and encourage greater interest on the part of students in this emerging area. It is particularly gratifying to note that this special issue contains work from several different regions and work of the highest academic quality and rigour. Contributions such as these serve not only to bolster extant research in the field, but also to remind colleagues of the value and significance of such work. Without such contributions, I fear our marketing colleagues will continue to regard our realm in a manner that must be avoided at all costs-with consummate indifference.

Adrian Sargeant
Chair-Centre for Voluntary Sector Management
Henley Management College
Greenlands, Henley-On-Thames, Oxon RG9 3AU
adrians@henleymc.ac.uk

Introduction

Marketing is under fire. The challenges fall into several categories but include questions about the costs of marketing and the consumerist values that marketing is perceived to promote. Calls for legislation and regulation to counter alleged marketing "abuses" are becoming more strident (Day and Montgomery, 1999). Marketers must address these issues and articulate more effectively the discipline's multi-faceted contributions to society. Ironically it is now more than three decades since Kotler and Levy (1969) advanced the then-controversial propositions that *all* organizations must develop a marketing function to fulfil their responsibilities to stakeholders and that commercial marketing methods and concepts are transferable to the nonprofit sector. Most marketing theorists and practitioners have long since accepted the notion of social marketing but we have been less than adept at communicating the concept to others. When asked *What does marketing contribute to society?* emphasizing the role of social marketing should be our primary response.

Social marketing is generally understood to involve the planning and implementation of programs designed to bring about social change using concepts from commercial marketing. As a rapidly emerging discipline, social marketing is demonstrating considerable success in tapping the ideas and talents of commercial marketers to challenge major social problems through partnerships of mutual interest. Social marketers are achieving results for a myriad of philanthropic organizations, community groups, and government agencies around the world engaged in solving social problems.

Allied to (or a sub-set of) social marketing is a fairly recent phenomenon known as "Cause Related Marketing" (see for example

[Haworth co-indexing entry note]: "Introduction." Ewing, Michael T. Co-published simultaneously in *Journal of Nonprofit & Public Sector Marketing* (Best Business Books, an imprint of The Haworth Press, Inc.) Vol. 9, No. 4, 2001, pp. 1-4 ; and: *Social Marketing* (ed: Michael T. Ewing) Best Business Books, an imprint of The Haworth Press, Inc., 2001, pp. 1-4. Single or multiple copies of this article are available for a fee from The Haworth Document Delivery Service [1-800-HAWORTH, 9:00 a.m. - 5:00 p.m. (EST). E-mail address: getinfo@haworthpressinc.com].

Varadarajan and Menon, 1988). In their recent book *Brand Spirit*, Pringle and Thompson (1999) define Cause Related Marketing as a strategic positioning and marketing tool which links a company or brand to a relevant social cause or issue for mutual benefit. Already, organizations such as Andrex, American Express, Avon, BMW, the Body Shop, Kelloggs, Liz Claiborne, Marks & Spencer, McDonald's, Proctor & Gamble, Reebok and many others have embraced social and cause related marketing in one way or another, yet scholarly treatment of the subject remains scant and eclectic. Fortunately, academe has recognised the urgent need for empirical research in this area, and it is especially encouraging to see that four well-established, refereed marketing journals have recently dedicated special issues to social marketing-related themes.

While three of these publications are still in print, I am sure they will be well received and hope that they will complement this special issue, which contains five diverse contributions: Diverse in terms of topics, methodologies, author nationalities and even philosophical/ideological positions. The lead article by Hutton ignites some controversy. It is a thought-provoking conceptual piece on the misapplication of marketing to major (American) social institutions. He considers whether marketing as a force for social *dis*order may have become a reality and questions the applicability of the customer metaphor, which is so central to marketing, to productive social institutions. While I am generally an admirer of Hutton's work, I personally do not share his desire to narrow the scope of marketing. I do, however, respect his views and challenge other interested scholars to take up this debate (i.e., is the scope of marketing becoming too broad?).

The second article, by the Mizerski's and Sadler, compares and contrasts the comparative effectiveness of a CRM program with "ambush" advertising for social causes by exploring whether a social cause needs to be naturally associated with a cause sponsor. Findings suggest that an ambush social cause appeal can perform just as well as a CRM appeal, and that a social cause need not be closely associated to the marketer to favorably influence perceptions of the audience.

Pitt and his colleagues transfer the focus from established to emerging media by investigating donations to charity and donor motivations. Why do individuals donate time, money and other resources to charities? While marketers and social scientists have for some time explained donation and gift giving in terms of the exchange paradigm, consumer researchers have recently introduced the notion of agapic (or unselfish) behavior to explain aspects of donor motivation. Using the case of a successful charitable Internet site, Hungersite.com, Pitt et al. contrast the exchange and agapic paradigms of donation behavior and discuss the strategic implications this may have for charity marketing strategy.

Caruana and Chircop take a macro view. They explore the "darker side" of globalization and liberalization, and the processes that may be fostering feelings of helplessness and alienation among affected communities worldwide. The main aim of their study is to consider the possibility that anomia or feelings of helplessness and alienation are correlated to ethnocentrism. Drawing on the findings of survey, they offer some preliminary implications for theory and policy development in this under-researched domain.

Finally, McMahon offers a useful overview of recent developments in social marketing in a global context and discusses the relationship of these developments to those in commercial marketing and public relations. He then relates the global context to developments in Australasia, with particular reference to social engineering during economic restructuring. Personally, I think that McMahon has touched on an extremely important topic, and I see the issue of social marketing versus social engineering as being a key imperative for future research, perhaps coupled with an investigation of "nanny states" versus stakeholder societies.

As I mentioned earlier, this special issue of *Journal of Nonprofit & Public Sector Marketing* presents five diverse, high-quality articles, for which I would like to thank the contributing authors. I would also like to thank the journal's co-editors, Don Self and Walter Wymer, for their assistance and encouragement over the years. Finally, I am indebted to the reviewers who selflessly gave up their valuable time to make invaluable contributions to this project. Consistent with journal policy, a double-blind review process was followed, resulting in a final acceptance rate of 35%. I would therefore like to acknowledge the submissions I received but was not able to include:

SPECIAL ISSUE REVIEWERS

Pierre Berthon
Bentley College

Keith Blois
Oxford University

Stephen Brown
University of Ulster

Albert Caruana
University of Malta

Nigel de Bussy
Curtin University of Technology

Barbara A. Lafferty
University of South Florida

Elaine Leong
Edith Cowan University

Gerard Prendergast
Hong Kong Baptist University

Arthur Money
Henley Management College

B. Ramaseshan
Curtin University of Technology

Marie Murgolo-Poore
Curtin University of Technology

Adrian Sargeant
Henley Management College

Julie Napoli
Curtin University of Technology

Douglas West
Westminster University

Michael T. Ewing
Editor

REFERENCES

Day, G.S. and Montgomery, D.B. (1999), Charting New Directions for Marketing. *Journal of Marketing*, 63, (Special Issue): 3-13.

Kotler, P. and Levy, S. (1969), Broadening the Concept of Marketing. *Journal of Marketing*, 33, (January), 10-15.

Pringle, H. and Thompson, M. (1999), *Brand Spirit. How Cause Related Marketing Builds Brands.* John Wiley & Sons: Chichester, England.

Varadarajan, P.R. and Menon, A. (1988), Cause-Related Marketing: A Coalignment of Marketing Strategy and Corporate Philanthropy. *Journal of Marketing*, 52, 3, 58-75.

Narrowing the Concept
of Marketing

James G. Hutton

SUMMARY. The misapplication of marketing to major American social institutions-education, religion, health care, the media, government
and the legal system-has frequently undermined the fundamental pur-
poses of those institutions, to the point that Laczniak and Michie's
(1979a; 1979b) worst fears about marketing as a force for social disorder
may have become a reality. Even more perplexing is a deeper question
that marketers have yet to address adequately: Is the customer metaphor,
which is so central to business and consumer marketing, fundamentally
incompatible with the nature of a productive social institution? *[Article
copies available for a fee from The Haworth Document Delivery Service:
1-800-HAWORTH. E-mail address: <getinfo@haworthpressinc.com> Website:
<http://www.HaworthPress.com> © 2001 by The Haworth Press, Inc. All rights re-
served.]*

KEYWORDS. Misapplication, social disorder, customer metaphor,
productive social institution

James G. Hutton is Associate Professor, Fairleigh Dickinson University, 1000
River Road-H-DH2-07, Teaneck, NJ 07601 (E-mail: hutton@alpha.fdu.edu; personal
web page http://alpha.fdu.edu/~hutton). He has a PhD in marketing from the University of Texas at Austin, and conducts research in areas such as brand equity, relationship marketing and (integrated) marketing communications.

The author thanks the Samuel J. Silberman College of Business Administration at
Fairleigh Dickinson University for financial support of this research.

[Haworth co-indexing entry note]: "Narrowing the Concept of Marketing." Hutton, James G. Co-published simultaneously in *Journal of Nonprofit & Public Sector Marketing* (Best Business Books, an imprint of
The Haworth Press, Inc.) Vol. 9, No. 4, 2001, pp. 5-24; and: *Social Marketing* (ed: Michael T. Ewing) Best
Business Books, an imprint of The Haworth Press, Inc., 2001, pp. 5-24. Single or multiple copies of this article
are available for a fee from The Haworth Document Delivery Service [1-800-HAWORTH, 9:00 a.m. - 5:00
p.m. (EST). E-mail address: getinfo@haworthpressinc.com].

5

INTRODUCTION

In evaluating social and cause-related marketing, it's appropriate for both scholars and practitioners to step back and consider basic questions about the context and the appropriateness of such marketing tactics:

- Is cause-related marketing simply a cynical exploitation of public sympathies for the sake of profits?
- If the idea of being a good corporate citizen is to be sincere and meaningful, shouldn't philanthropic activities be divorced entirely from profit-making activities?
- Isn't social marketing sometimes of questionable social value, to the extent that one person's cause is another person's propaganda?

The foremost question raised by this article is even deeper and perhaps more radical: Is a marketing or customer orientation fundamentally inappropriate for social institutions (schools, churches, charitable organizations and the like), which are the most common beneficiaries of social and cause-related marketing?

THE BROADENING CONTROVERSY

To help answer the question, it's useful to revisit the "broadening" controversy of 30 years ago, which began with publication of Kotler and Levy's (1969a) landmark article, "Broadening the Concept of Marketing." Essentially, the article argued that marketing should move beyond the domain of traditional economic products and services, and into the realm of non-business products and services such as health care, education, political elections, churches, foundations, museums and social causes. Kotler and Levy's premise was that "marketing is a pervasive social activity." A sometimes heated debate ensued, concerning the appropriate scope and nature of marketing as both an academic and applied discipline (see Arndt, 1978; Barksdale, 1979; Kotler, 1973; Kotler & Levy, 1969b). Some argued that marketing was being broadened too far (Luck, 1969) or should be deepened, as well as-or in lieu of-being broadened (Enis, 1973). Bartels (1974) described the debate as an "identity crisis" in which it was unclear whether marketing should be defined by the subject matter with which it dealt or by the technology and techniques by which it is handled.

In "A Generic Concept of Marketing" (1972), Kotler elaborated and refined the basic concepts of a broadened concept of marketing. The centerpiece of that article was a series of metaphors describing the new "products" and "customers" that were to be the focus of a broadened concept of marketing:

Organization	Product	Customer
Museum	Cultural appreciation	General public
National Safety Council	Safer driving	Driving public
Political candidate	Honest government	Voting public
Family Planning Foundation	Birth control	Fertile public
Police department	Safety	General public
Church	Religious experience	Church members
University	Education	Students

Unfortunately, the profound implications of those metaphors were never fully explored or debated in forums outside the marketing field. Perhaps even more unfortunately, the general "customer" metaphor (student-as-customer, religious follower-as-customer, art patron-as-customer and so forth) found its way into the lexicon of public institutions.

In hindsight, it appears that the indiscriminate broadening of marketing over the past few decades has been a major force in the transformation of the character of American institutions-and the character of Americans. What might be described as the misapplication of marketing to major American social institutions may have eroded their purpose and integrity in fundamental ways, to the point that Laczniak and Michie's (1979a; 1979b) worst fears about marketing as a force for social disorder may have become a reality. If so, marketers and marketing scholars have a collective opportunity and responsibility to revisit the issue, trace its evolution and causes, identify its fundamental tenets, communicate its dangers, and articulate a remedy. In short, it may be time to *narrow* the concept of marketing.

OF CITIZENSHIP, VICTIMIZATION, MATERIALISM AND ADDICTION

One might argue that Kotler and Levy were simply describing an evolutionary process that was already decades or centuries old, and that they deserve a relatively modest share of the credit (or blame) for events that followed. Nonetheless, their work called attention to an important trend that seemed to accelerate dramatically in the following two or three decades.

Ewen (1989) touched on the crux of the issue when he observed that everywhere American society once used the word "citizen," over the past few decades it has substituted the word "consumer." The implication of his observation seems to explain much of what is happening currently in American society: As citizens, Americans had rights and responsibilities; as consumers, they have rights but few, if any, responsibilities.

Sykes (1993), among others, addressed this issue from a similar perspective, lamenting the passing of the term "citizen" and the concept of citizenship from the public vernacular, and the resulting rise of the U.S. as what he called "a nation of victims." Sykes attributed the death of citizenship to an amalgam of influences, most notably the civil rights movement of the 1960s, the women's movement, rampant litigation caused by too many lawyers chasing too few real injustices, a newfound immaturity in Americans' intellectual growth as a people, and the rise of what he referred to as the "therapeutic culture," in which virtually any behavioral shortcoming or character flaw can be-and has been-elevated to the status of a disease or syndrome over which individuals have no control or responsibility.

While Sykes' argument was interesting, it appears that those conditions were not the primary *force*, but the *context* in which a more overarching force was at work. The self-serving interests of lawyers, therapists and various victims (some real, some imagined) may have created a fertile climate for an assault on citizenship, but it appears to be a more fundamental cultural change-cutting across all political and special-interest groups-that is the malady itself. Namely, post-modern America is a culture of consumption, as Ewen suggested, in which we have been transformed from citizens into customers or consumers.

Fox and Lears (1982), among others, provided insightful glimpses into the new American consumer culture, which supersedes the *therapeutic* and other subcultures described by Sykes. One of the important characteristics of that consumer culture is that its potential dangers extend well beyond critics' traditional concerns about the moral, political and ecological consequences of materialism. While Twitchell (1999), Star (1989) and many others have lamented the spiritual and environmental dangers of marketers constantly pitching products and services that consumers want but don't necessarily need, the consumer-metaphor's invasion of social institutions has created a new dimension of concern. Institutions like churches and schools, which traditionally upheld intellectual and moral standards by aspiring to give people what they needed, rather than what they wanted, are now doing just the opposite, in many cases, causing many to question whether they have abandoned their fundamental social responsibility and raison d'être.

In fairness to the advocates of a broadened concept of marketing, it is important to point out that the original "broadening" concept was, at least to some extent, refined and embedded in a foundation of social responsibility (see Levy & Kotler, 1979). Nonetheless, some of the early rhetoric of the movement, in the hands of amateur marketers or marketers unwilling or unable to see the potential abuses of this potent new medicine, became more like the boastful claims of an elixir.

In fact, the metaphor of a drug (or patent medicine) is quite fitting. The early "broadening" advocates were in some ways analogous to author Ken Kesey, who was one of the guinea pigs of early U.S. government experiments with the hallucinogen LSD (see Kesey, 1968). Recognizing the power but also the limitations of such drugs, Kesey admonished his followers to go "beyond" acid (a.k.a. LSD). Similarly, Kotler's later writings spelled out the need for a less literal and more enlightened view of how schools, churches and other nonprofit organizations should be marketed. Kotler (1988) also advocated a more humanistic approach to marketing, in general. Among other things, he suggested the need to go "beyond" the marketing concept to a "societal" marketing concept. However, just as Kesey's warnings were largely ignored by his followers (who became ground zero for a new drug culture that spread throughout the U.S.), Kotler and Levy's message of responsible use of the marketing concept largely fell on deaf ears, leaving a trail of consumer "addicts" in its wake.

INSTITUTIONS UNDER FIRE

A review of American social institutions reveals the dramatic impact made by the misapplication of the marketing concept.

Education: Students as Customers

Perhaps the field of education best illustrates the impact of marketing on social institutions. Laying all of the problems in American education at the feet of marketing is clearly unfair. Postman (1985), for example, suggested that television is much to blame. Nonetheless, an examination of the state of American education from a marketing perspective appears to explain much of what is happening in the nation's schools. Indeed, it appears that most of the key issues being debated in American primary and secondary education-including school choice, vouchers, charter schools, commercialization of the classroom and for-profit management of public schools-are either directly or indirectly related to marketing.

More important is the new attitude of American students. Many-perhaps most-students believe they are consumers of education. Critics argue that the atmosphere of American schools-with their exclusive marketing agreements with food and beverage companies, corporate-sponsored "education" kits, and advertising-sponsored television shows beamed into classes-is teaching children that everything has a price and everything is fodder for a marketing tie-in. School children-along with their parents-are further encouraged to regard themselves as buyers and consumers of education by state and school-district laws and policies (e.g., vouchers, magnet schools) that increasingly allocate resources based on the number of students a school attracts. Even some educators have encouraged students to regard themselves as consumers of education (e.g., Rothschild & White, 1993).

Besides raising questions about materialism, work ethic and personal responsibility, the student-as-customer mentality may underlie other issues of concern in American education. The self-esteem movement that is now entrenched in American education, for example, perhaps can be explained best in terms of marketing: Neither the student-customer nor the parents are ever to be offended because "the customer is always right." The movement has manifested itself in a variety of ways, including so-called social promotion of under-qualified students and the elimination of class ranking from students' transcripts. The results include denial and an inflated sense of self. While American school children had the highest perception of how well they had done in the Third International Mathematical and Science Study (1997), they actually ranked near the bottom in almost all categories.

Viewed in terms of either educational theory or basic psychology, it is difficult to imagine how self-esteem can be built without standards, self-discipline or honest criticism and feedback. In fact, the self-esteem philosophy prevalent in American education appears to be a prescription for delaying student maturity and *destroying* self-esteem. It might be argued that failure is, in many ways, at the heart of education, in the sense that each child should push him- or herself ever higher, often to the point of failure, from which the student then rebounds and conquers the higher task on the next try or the one after that. When children are never allowed to fail, however, a cornerstone of the education process has been taken away.

At the college level, where students have many more choices, schools have responded to the increasingly competitive environment by sprinkling their recruiting materials with customer-oriented language, adopting various customer-focused philosophies, and even making outright declarations that "students are our customers." While those words and ideas may sound appealing to potential students and their parents, they are ultimately self-defeating. For one thing, those ideas confuse accountability with customer service.

Even if one were to buy into the notion of educational customers, it is unclear exactly what or who the "product" and "customer" are. Some may cling to Kotler and Levy's (1969a) notion that the product is education, but one might just as easily argue that students, themselves, are the product, and that employers, benefactors and taxpayers are actually the customers, given that government and foundation grants, employer tuition reimbursements, donations and citizens' tax dollars pay for the bulk of universities' expenses. Others might argue for a variety of other metaphors (e.g., students as members of a network or a club, in the case of elite schools). Ultimately, however, it appears that the proper metaphor is simply "student"-a unique and appropriate designation for those seeking an education rather than buying a degree.

Beyond the practical difficulties of treating students (or their parents or their employers or the community) as customers of education are the fundamental philosophical contradictions that it creates. Hartoonian (1997) suggested that the student-as-customer metaphor was completely backwards, insofar as education should be about teaching students that they are *producers*, not consumers. Students who believe they are customers assume they can come to class as they please; that student evaluations of teachers are tantamount to customer-evaluation forms; and that grades and an education are things to be bought rather than earned. Students who see themselves as producers or citizens, on the other hand, feel they have rights, but also obligations to the institution and to the larger community.

Ideally, the goal of society should be to educate students to think broadly and deeply about issues that affect all people. Students who see themselves as consumers tend to behave in exactly the opposite manner-thinking narrowly and shallowly about only themselves. In so doing, they defy what Cicero described as the fundamental purpose of an education: to free ourselves from the tyranny of the present.

Journalism: Readers and Viewers as Customers

No less a concern than formal education is the *continuing* education of the citizenry, a function largely performed in the United States by mass media. Traditionally, the credo of most major newsrooms was focused principally on truth-seeking and truth-telling, as a means of arming the citizenry with information necessary to participate in a democratic society. In some cases, editors claimed to be telling people "not what to think, but what to think *about*." In other cases, editors described their jobs as "comforting the afflicted and afflicting the comfortable." In perhaps the most enlightened view, Walter Lippman (1922) described the purpose of journalism as helping people cope with their world. Whether those philosophies and credos were actually practiced by the media as a whole is of some dispute (witness the earlier periods of "yellow journalism" in American history), but those who have been around journalism for many years can attest to the dramatic changes in most newsrooms, in terms of the growing marketing and customer orientation on the editorial side, as well as the business side of the media.

Among the many complaints of reporters and editors: a dumbing-down of news to pander to audiences; increased focus on scandal, sex and violence; increased conflicts of interest between the news and editorial sides of the media, including favorable treatment of sister companies within large media conglomerates; kid-glove treatment of advertisers; increasingly blurred lines between entertainment and hard news; and a decline in "enterprise" reporting (where reporters initiate stories, rather than relying on news releases or pitches generated by PR and marketing departments and agencies).

In short, it has become painfully apparent to most serious journalists and editors, in all media, that the purpose of journalism today is primarily *to package audiences for advertisers*. That is a vastly different goal than traditionally espoused, and one that is sometimes diametrically opposed to the ideals of journalism.

Government: Citizens as Customers

Needless to say, marketing's impact on American politics has been profound. While some consider William McKinley's 1896 presidential campaign to be the first to use the gamut of marketing and publicity techniques-including advertising, press releases, trained speakers, billboards, posters and millions of fliers printed in nine languages (Thayer, 1974)-most historians consider John Kennedy to be the first U.S. president to make optimum use of modern media and marketing techniques. Lyndon Johnson's "daisy" ad during the 1964 election brought political advertising to a new level, in exploiting the American public's fear that challenger Barry Goldwater had an itchy trigger-finger when it came to the use of nuclear weapons. Richard Nixon, assisted by former advertising executive H. R. Haldeman and other marketing and media experts, raised the stakes even higher. Ronald Reagan brought a new combination of theater and marketing to the White House, through his team's use of focus groups, public-opinion polling, "speech pulsing" (to measure the impact of debates and speeches), and coordinated ads and promotional films (e.g., the classic campaign film, "Morning in America"). Bush and Clinton, it appears, carried on the tradition.

Less visible than campaign marketing, but at least as important to American government and policy, has been the marketing of a variety of public programs. Franklin Roosevelt may have laid the groundwork with an overt marketing campaign for his New Deal, but later programs would be much subtler and more sophisticated. Smith (1983), for example, offered an insightful behind-the-scenes look at how NASA sold the space program to the American public, sometimes sacrificing scientific considerations for marketing considerations.

An even more telling example, perhaps, has been the government's marketing of war. The use of myths, symbols, slogans and various marketing techniques have always been an integral part of war, of course. The nature of the marketing of wars seems to have changed significantly in recent decades, however, in terms of both quality and quantity. With the Persian Gulf War, we saw what might have been the world's first war with its own brand name ("Desert Storm") and logotype. That war's imagery also evoked new metaphors of war as sport (as we counted the number of SCUD-missile hits versus misses), war as action-adventure show (with TV reporters acting as hosts of the nightly show) and war as video game (as Americans watched surreal videos of one of their missiles descending on an enemy target, and another of American missile descending on one of its own military vehicles in a horrifying friendly-fire accident). Filmmaker Barry Levinson's biting satire, *Wag the Dog*, added another new metaphor-war as distraction.

Attempts by governments to commercialize, privatize and market everything from education to health care to welfare to prisons demands further historical reflection, according to Kuttner (see Black, 1997):

> The attempt to lionize the market and debase political democracy is very, very dangerous. It reminds one in a slightly more benign way of the '20s and '30s, when the totalitarian countries ridiculed the democracies as too weak and too divided. This is more subtle and more insidious, because it's being perpetrated by people who think of themselves as champions of free choice but who impeach the idea that we can be a self-governing and free people.
>
> Free-market ideologues like to imply that freedom in the market inevitably leads to freedom in society. But they overlook the many instances . . . such as fascist Italy and Germany in the 1930s, in which capitalism coexisted with the most repressive political and social systems imaginable. [Kuttner points out that today one need only look as far as China for an example of a nation that seems determined to demonstrate, once again, that free markets can exist without free people.]
>
> For the sake of civil society, for the sake of political democracy, there needs to be a realm that is off limits to the market.

Religion: Followers as Customers

Perhaps more than any other American institution, religious organizations have sought to resist the allure of marketing (e.g., Kenneson, Street & Hauerwas, 1997). Yet even here, the effects of marketing seem to be everywhere (see Roof, 1994, and Wuthnow, 1998, for overviews of U.S. religious life in recent decades). In many Protestant congregations, virtually every aspect of church life-who is hired as minister, when and how services are held, what music is played, how members are recruited, etc.-is now influenced by marketing considerations.

Belk, Wallendorf and Sherry (1989) were among the first to describe the secularization of religion and, conversely, the sacralization of the secular in modern American life. In America's spiritual marketplace, consumers can choose from more than 2,000 distinct religious groups (Niebuhr, 1997). The New Age protestant and nondenominational organizations have drawn most of the attention, with their drive-in churches, focus groups, direct-marketing campaigns and mall-style programs that pander to just about every conceivable desire. The most traditional religions, however, have joined the act, as well.

Even on the surface, the application of marketing to religion raises some discomforting questions. For example, should a church with significant "brand equity" create "line extensions" to cater to specific segments of the market, to expand its total "market share"? They are not moot questions. Indeed, many churches are embracing precisely that terminology and mindset. The Southern Baptist Convention's much-publicized proposal to target Jews for conversion raised more than a few eyebrows, and has brought the "market share" issue into the open.

At a deeper level, a question arises not only about whether such marketing may taint churches in some way, but about whether such marketing is antithetical to the basic tenets of most religions, and to the very purpose of most churches. Traditional notions of fear, guilt, responsibility, delayed gratification, sacrifice and service often seem to fall victim to self-defined notions of spirituality, immediacy and self-esteem:

> The heart of the gospel is being assaulted. All this is, is a religious version of self-help. The Christian faith that is emerging from these churches . . . has been reduced to what makes you feel a little less anxious or a bit better about yourself. It's replacing a self-centered, self-focused type of Christianity for what we have in the Bible, which is . . . God-centered. (Housewright, 1995)

Or, as the director of continuing education at Duke Divinity School put it, a church is not supposed to be a place that makes us feel comfortable with who we are, but "a place where we're transformed by God's grace into something we're not" (Long, 1993).

Health Care: Patients as Customers

The marketing of health care raises still other critical issues about the marketing of institutions. As a philosophical matter, Davidson (1996) pointed out that the marketing of health care lacks at least two conditions essential for the fair, efficient functioning of a market: (a) more-or-less equal standing of buyer and seller, who come together in an open exchange process, and (b) open access to knowledge on the part of both buyer and seller.

In the first case, Davidson points out that the exchange process in health care is far removed from the straightforward buyer-seller or manufacturer-retailer-customer models of marketing. To illustrate, he uses the example of a patient's purchase of a prescription drug:

First, the product must be prescribed by a physician. Second, the payer may well be an insurance company. Third, the drugstore's pharmacist may influence the choice between branded or generic products. And fourth, the Food and Drug Administration (FDA) exercises tight control over the entire industry. This complex model distorts the exchange process almost beyond recognition.

In terms of the requirement of more-or-less equal standing of buyer and seller, it is worth noting, too, that health maintenance organizations cannot be sued, under current U.S. law, contributing to a lack of accountability and an imbalance in power.

In the second case (access to knowledge), the imbalance between buyer and seller is even greater-and not by accident. While economists perpetually reiterate that perfect or near-perfect knowledge is a fundamental requirement for the proper functioning of markets, the health care system in the United States works continually to prevent consumers from obtaining that knowledge. To cite just one example, the American Medical Association (AMA) has sought to abolish the National Practitioner Data Bank, a federally run agency that keeps records of doctors' malpractice-lawsuit histories, which was begun in 1990 to prevent unscrupulous doctors from skipping state-to-state without being found out. Despite efforts to open the database to the public, information is accessible only to hospitals and other groups that employ physicians.

As a practical matter, few would argue that the commercialization of health care in the U.S., in general, has been productive for the average American (Herzlinger, 1997). From the consumer's perspective, the promise of "health maintenance organizations" (which were originally sold to the American public as organizations designed to promote better health through preventive medicine) has turned out to be largely a myth. Most health-care consumers find it more difficult to get needed *chronic* care under managed-care organizations, much less *preventive* care. The problem has become so acute that in 1998 President Clinton proposed a patient bill-of-rights (which Congress debated in 1999) to help protect citizens from the abuses of managed care.

Accusations and investigations of one of the country's largest health care organizations, Columbia/HCA Healthcare, called attention to some of the potential dangers of the patient-as-customer mentality of such organizations. Among the accusations: above-average costs (despite claims of cheaper, more efficient health care); financial incentives to do unnecessary surgeries; commissions or finders' fees for doctors who direct patients to company-owned hospitals; and rejection of "bad" patients (i.e., those unable to pay). (See Malhotra & Miller, 1996, for a general discussion of ethics in managed health care.)

Lest all the blame fall on doctors, pharmaceutical manufacturers and HMOs, it is worth noting that independent hospitals have also engaged in some dubious practices that are based on marketing considerations. For example, there have already been reports that certain hospitals have essentially declined to admit certain "difficult" cases because their failure rate (often defined by the hospital's mortality rate) would suffer, thereby hurting the statistics that are featured in their advertising.

A final example of the dangers of marketing in the healthcare arena is the prescription of antibiotics in the United States. Researchers at the Centers for Disease Control and Prevention (CDC) estimate that as many as a third of the approximately 150 million courses of antibiotic treatment each year may be unnecessary. Doctors write roughly a million antibiotic prescriptions a year for *viral* infections, knowing full well that not only are antibiotics ineffective against viral infections, but also that such indiscriminate use of antibiotics can lower both the individual's and the broader community's resistance to bacteria-based infections. It is difficult to say what was in the minds of all of those doctors, but it appears likely that a large percentage of those prescriptions were written to keep patients happy. While that may be good for customer relations, it is a direct violation of doctors' Hippocratic oath-to do no harm.

The Legal System: Judges and Juries as Customers

"The entire legal system is upside down," according to comedian Dennis Miller. "We have people's lives being determined by 12 people in a room whose main goal in life is to wrap it up and get home in time to watch reruns." Mark Twain (1872) made a similar observation of a murder case in which anybody who had read the newspaper was disqualified from the jury: "The system rigidly excludes men of brains."

Twain likely could not have imagined, however, the lengths to which present-day lawyers would use modern marketing techniques and consultants to try to subvert the supposed objective of impartiality in seating a jury and to try to tilt jurors' biases in their clients' favor. Jury consultants all over the country are using focus groups, "shadow" juries, mock trials, databases, and psychographic and demographic profiling to test-market their clients' cases. A Florida firm, for example, has used something called "PercepTrac" to track responses to jury arguments based on age, income and psychographic profile (Schwartz, 1993).

Long before the conclusion of O. J. Simpson's murder trial, most criminal defense lawyers predicted correctly that Simpson would walk out of the Los Angeles courtroom a free man. There is a growing consensus, in fact, that most trials, especially lengthy trials, really are decided during jury selection. In the mid-1980s, a Philadelphia assistant prosecutor created a how-to videotape for prosecutors that illustrated, step-by-step, how to seat a "good" (i.e., ignorant, not-too-bright, biased) jury. Among other things, he advised his colleagues to exclude young blacks from juries because they would be much less likely to convict. The assistant prosecutor labeled as "ridiculous" the ideal of seating a jury that is "competent, fair and impartial": "The only way you're going to do your best is to get jurors that are unfair and more likely to convict than anybody else" (*New York Times*, 1997).

A SUMMARY OF THE ISSUES

In summary, it might be said that the inappropriate application of marketing to American social institutions (especially the use of the customer metaphor) has not only helped to subvert their fundamental roles and objectives, in many cases, but in some instances may actually be helping to accomplish objectives that are diametrically opposed to the ideals of those institutions.

- Whereas education's classical goal was to develop individuals who would think broadly and deeply about issues affecting all of humankind, student-customers are encouraged to think (if at all) narrowly and shallowly about themselves.
- Whereas health care's traditional ideal placed the patient first, the marketing of health care has helped put profits ahead of people.
- Whereas most American religions were traditionally God-centered organizations designed to help transform followers into a new state of enlightenment and service, the marketing of religion has helped create self-centered organizations in which follower-customers are encouraged to feel comfortable with whomever and whatever they are.
- Whereas a traditional ideal of the justice system was to produce unbiased juries of one's peers, the application of marketing to the legal system has helped produce an environment in which the ob-

jective is to produce juries that are as biased as possible, with judges and juries serving as customers of legal cases that have been developed through test marketing.

- Whereas the traditional ideal of journalism was to help readers and viewers cope with their world by delivering unbiased information and truth about important issues, the application of marketing to journalism and the media has resulted in reader-, listener- and viewer-customers being offered whatever will help lure them into the fold, so they can be packaged and sold to advertisers.
- Whereas the traditional ideals of government included public service and moral leadership, the marketing of politics and politicians has helped create a new and disturbing era of propaganda in which even the most educated members of the intelligentsia have a difficult time sorting through the daily maze of politicians' lies, photo-ops and spin-doctoring, in which politicians are remade almost weekly in the image of the latest public-opinion poll, and in which the notion of war as theater (with citizens of various nations as customers of war) does not seem far-fetched at all.

CONCLUSIONS

While some may argue that marketing has always been a force in the realm of American social institutions, the current popularity of marketing within those institutions appears to be unprecedented, in several important respects. Many schools, churches and hospitals that would have been extremely uncomfortable in discussing their activities in marketing terms, even a few decades ago, now fully embrace marketing terminology and mindsets. The customer metaphor has become so pervasive that many Americans-especially younger Americans-have developed a keen sense of entitlement and have difficulty thinking of themselves in terms *other* than marketing (e.g., as citizens). The public dialog surrounding institutions has changed in fundamental ways, to the point that marketing and market forces are deemed the best-or perhaps the only-solution to a wide variety of public dilemmas ranging from dysfunctional public schools to crumbling prison systems.

Thirty years after the call for a "broadened" concept of marketing, there is little doubt that marketing has substantially increased its role in the day-to-day operation of social institutions, and fundamentally altered the mindset of those institutions. Whether that greater influence has been for the betterment of society, however, is debatable. Among the possible positions one might hold:

- Marketing is, indeed, a pervasive social activity, and its application to social institutions is entirely appropriate, without restraint.
- Social institutions are inherently different than strictly for-profit organizations, and therefore marketing philosophies and techniques should be applied with caution and some restraint.
- Marketing philosophies are appropriate in the context of social institutions, but specific marketing concepts may be inappropriate (e.g., market share, in the case of churches; focus groups, in the case of jury selection; or customer satisfaction, the case of schools).
- Marketing philosophies and concepts are inherently incompatible with the nature of properly functioning social institutions.

This paper argues for a position that falls somewhere between the last two philosophies. Specifically, it defines the "misapplication" of marketing to social institutions as the application of marketing philosophies, strategies or tactics whenever they serve to:

- help give people what they *want* at the expense of what they *need*, usurping the fundamental moral responsibility of the institution (e.g., when doctors prescribe antibiotics, knowing that they are inappropriate, for the sake of keeping patients happy);
- substitute a "customer" mentality for a more appropriate metaphor (e.g., when students are encouraged to think of themselves as customers rather than citizens or students); or
- undermine the fundamental tenets or purpose of an institution (e.g., when churches substitute more-marketable concepts like self-gratification for defining principles such as sacrifice and selflessness).

If one agrees with these propositions, a further question arises: To what extent are marketing scholars (or even practitioners) morally and professionally obligated to publicly engage in dialog about marketing's potential dangers (or damage already inflicted) in the context of social institutions?

One implication for marketing scholars is the need for further reflection, historical analysis and theory development. Carmen (1980), for example, reviewed all of the basic marketing paradigms of the time, and then put forth a theoretical framework that effectively excluded such institutions as politics and religion from the domain of marketing.

Marketing scholars probably would be wise to dig even deeper, returning to the discipline's roots, in the field of economics, to help determine the nature of contemporary markets and how far the notion of markets and marketing should be extended. De Long and Froomkin (1998), for example, question whether our traditional notions of a market apply equally well, if at all, in a service economy, much less in an information economy. If their assertions are true-that we as a society need to redefine some of our most basic ideas about markets-a logical conclusion is that both marketing scholars and practitioners might also need to redefine some of their most basic ideas about marketing.

At the same time, interestingly, contemporary biographers and historians have questioned whether our traditional notions about the nature of markets are even historically accurate. For example, in the process of writing about the life, times and business exploits of John D. Rockefeller, Sr., Chernow (1998) rediscovered that American history's most renowned capitalist was not really a proponent of capitalism, or at least the kind of free-market capitalism that most people think about today. Rockefeller actually acted and sounded much more like a Marxist. One of Chernow's conclusions was that "free markets don't exist in a state of nature. Free markets are things that have to be defined by custom and law" (see Murray, 1998).

Rule (1998, p. 35) came to a very similar conclusion:

> The "Market" doesn't exist. . . . Markets come in all forms and serve all sorts of interests. All of them are social creations. Only the most conscientious critical reflection can provide bases for deciding what domains of life should be governed by markets-and what form any such market should take.

Despite what he considered to be a serious lack of definition and understanding of what constitutes a market, Rule (1998, p. 29) made the case that "the market" is the central guiding principle of contemporary America:

> When historians of ideas go to work on the last decade of the twentieth century, the market will surely appear as one of our intellectual totems. What the Rights of Man were to the French Revolution-or what Manifest Destiny or the quest for the Kingdom of God on Earth were to their times-the market is to our own.

Another important question for scholars is the extent to which marketing's effects on social institutions may differ in other parts of the world. If one buys the argument that America's public institutions have been significantly affected by marketing's inroads into the realm of social institutions, to what extent are similar changes occurring elsewhere? Is the phenomenon a function of a unique brand of American materialism and consumerism, or does it apply to all developed economies?

Ultimately, the question of how far marketing should be broadened (or narrowed, as the case may be) depends largely on how one answers complementary questions about the nature of institutions and the nature of markets. In the 20th century, those questions were addressed primarily by the field of economics. In the 21st century, however, those questions are too important to be left to economists. In an age of production, economists should be among the most visible philosophers of a society; in an age of consumption, scholars of marketing and consumer behavior *should* be the preeminent philosophers. Ironically, however, it may be necessary for marketing scholars to narrow their concept of marketing in order to broaden their influence on society at large.

REFERENCES

Arndt, J. (1978). How broad should the marketing concept be? *Journal of Marketing*, *42* (January), 101-3.

Barksdale, H. C., Jr. (1979). The broadening controversy in marketing. In Franz, R. S., Hopkins, R. M., & Toma, A. G. (Eds.), *Proceedings of the annual conference of the Southern Marketing Association*, 456-9.

Bartels, R. (1974). The identity crisis in marketing. *Journal of Marketing*, *38* (October), 73-6.

Belk, R. W., Wallendorf, M., & Sherry, J. F., Jr. (1989). The sacred and the profane in consumer behavior: Theodicy on the odyssey. *Journal of Consumer Research*, *16* (June), 1-38.

Black, E. (1997, May 8). Everything's for sale, but at what price for society? *Star Tribune* (Minneapolis), p. A-22.

Carmen, J. M. (1980). Paradigms for marketing theory. In Jagdish N. Sheth (Ed.), *Research in marketing, Volume 3* (pp. 1-36). Greenwich, CT: JAI Press.

Chernow, R. (1998). *Titan: The life of John D. Rockefeller, Sr.* New York: Random House.

Davidson, K. (1996, December 2). Health care industries pose special ethics problems. *Marketing News*, p. 5.

De Long, J. B., & Froomkin, A. M. (1998). The next economy (working paper). University of California at Berkeley.

Enis, B. M. (1973). Deepening the concept of marketing. *Journal of Marketing, 37* (October), 57-62.

Ewen, S. (1989). As interviewed by Bill Moyers. In M. Collins (Ed.), *The public mind: Consuming images* (page 7 of transcript). New York: Public Affairs Television and Alvin H. Permutter, Inc.

Fox, R. W., & Lears, T. J. J. (Eds.) (1982). *The culture of consumption: Critical essays in American history, 1880-1980.* New York: Pantheon Books.

Hartoonian, M. (1997). Education is about producing, not consuming. *Social Education, 61(6),* 365-6.

Herzlinger, R. E. (1997). *Market-driven health care: Who wins, who loses in the transformation of America's largest service industry.* New York: Perseus Press.

Housewright, E. (1995, March 13). Do church ads work, or compromise gospel? *Marketing News,* p. 22.

Kenneson, P. D., Street, J. L., & Hauerwas, S. (1997). *Selling out the church: The dangers of church marketing.* Nashville, TN: Abingdon Press.

Kesey, K. (1968). *The electric kool-aid acid test.* New York: Bantam Books.

Kotler, P. (1972). A generic concept of marketing. *Journal of Marketing, 36* (April), 46-50.

_____ (1973). Defining the limits of marketing. In Becker, B. W., & Becker, H. (Eds.), *Combined proceedings of the American Marketing Association's winter and summer educators conferences* (pp. 48-56). Chicago: American Marketing Association.

_____ (1988). Humanistic marketing: Beyond the marketing concept. In Firat, A. F., Dholakia, N., & Bagozzi, R. (Eds.), *Philosophical and radical thought in marketing* (pp. 161-72). Lexington, MA: Lexington Books.

_____, & Levy, S. J. (1969a). Broadening the concept of marketing. *Journal of Marketing, 33* (January), 10-15.

_____ & _____ (1969b). A new form of marketing myopia: Rejoinder to Professor Luck. *Journal of Marketing, 33* (July), 55-7.

Laczniak, G. R., & Michie, D. A. (1979a). The social disorder of the broadened concept of marketing. *Journal of the Academy of Marketing Science,* 7 (summer), 214-32.

_____ & _____ (1979b). Broadened marketing and social disorder: A reply. *Journal of the Academy of Marketing Science,* 7 (summer), 239-41.

Levy, S. J., & Kotler, P. (1979). Toward a broader concept of marketing's role in social order (a rejoinder). *Journal of the Academy of Marketing Science,* 7 (summer), 233-41.

Lippman, W. (1922). *Public opinion.* New York: Harcourt, Brace and Co.

Long, S. (1993, April 12). As quoted in New church uses marketing to appeal to baby boomers. *Marketing News,* p. 11.

Luck, D. J. (1969). Broadening the concept of marketing-too far. *Journal of Marketing, 33* (July), 53-55.

Malhotra, N. K., & Miller, G. L. (1996). Ethical issues in marketing managed care. *Journal of Health Care Marketing, 16* (spring), 60-5.

Murray, A. (1998, May 18). Reading Rockefeller and busting up trusts. *Wall Street Journal,* p. 1.

New York Times (1997, April 4). Prosecutor's training film may be inmates' ticket to new trials, p. A-5.

Niebuhr, G. (1997, March 30). Death in a cult: The landscape; Land of religious freedom has universe of spirituality. *New York Times*, p. A-1.

Postman, N. (1985). Teaching as an amusing activity. In *Amusing ourselves to death* (pp. 142-54). New York: Penguin Books.

Roof, W. C. (1994). *A generation of seekers: The spiritual journeys of the baby boom generation*. San Francisco: Harper.

Rothschild, M., & White, L. (1993). The university in the market place: Some insights and some puzzles. In Clotfelter, C. T., & Rothschild, M. (Eds.), *Studies of supply and demand in higher education* (pp. 11-42). Chicago: University of Chicago Press.

Rule, J. B. (1998). Markets, in their place. *Dissent, 45* (winter), 29-35.

Schwartz, J. (1993, February). Marketing the verdict. *American Demographics*, pp. 52-5.

Smith, M. L. (1983). Selling the moon: The U.S. manned space program and the triumph of commodity scientism. In Fox, R. W., & Lears, T. J. J. (Eds.), *The culture of consumption: Critical essays in American history, 1880-1980* (pp. 175-209). New York: Pantheon Books.

Star, S. (1989). Marketing and its discontents. *Harvard Business Review* (November/December), 148-54.

Sykes, C. (1993). *A nation of victims*. New York: St. Martin's Press.

Thayer, G. (1974). *Who shakes the money tree? American campaign practices from 1789 to the present*. New York: Simon & Schuster.

Third international mathematics and science study (1997). Washington, D.C.: National Center for Education Statistics (report co-sponsored by the U.S. Department of Education and the National Science Foundation).

Twain, M. (1872). *Roughing it*. Hartford, CT: American Publishing Co.

Twitchell, J. B. (1999). *Lead us into temptation: The triumph of American materialism*. New York: Columbia University Press.

Wuthnow, R. (1998). *After heaven: Spirituality in America since the 1950s*. Berkeley, CA: University of California Press.

A Field Experiment
Comparing the Effectiveness of "Ambush"
and Cause Related Ad Appeals
for Social Marketing Causes

Dick Mizerski
Katherine Mizerski
Orin Sadler

SUMMARY. Cause related marketing (CRM) has changed corporate philanthropy into an alleged money maker for the corporate donor. While CRM requires a financial donation, tied to a sale, an "Ambush" causal marketer can potentially reap goodwill and sales without the financial cost of donating. This study uses a field experiment ad study (n = 459) to examine the comparative effectiveness of a true CRM *vs.* an Ambush ad approach for social causes. It also explores whether the chosen social cause needs to be naturally associated with the cause sponsor. The results suggest that an Ambush social cause appeal can perform as well as a CRM appeal, and that the social cause need not

---

Dick Mizerski, PhD, is Professor and Chair in Marketing, Head of School, Department of Information Management and Marketing, University of Western Australia, 35 Stirling Highway, Crawley, Western Australia 6009, Australia (E-mail: *dickm@ kroner.ecel.uwa.edu.au*).

Katherine Mizerski, PhD, is Senior Lecturer, School of Marketing, Tourism and Leisure, Edith Cowan University, Pearson Street, Churchlands, Western Australia, Australia.

Orin Sadler, PhD, formerly affiliated with Florida State, is retired.

[Haworth co-indexing entry note]: "A Field Experiment Comparing the Effectiveness of 'Ambush' and Cause Related Ad Appeals for Social Marketing Causes." Mizerski, Dick, Katherine Mizerski, and Orin Sadler. Co-published simultaneously in *Journal of Nonprofit & Public Sector Marketing* (Best Business Books, an imprint of The Haworth Press, Inc.) Vol. 9, No. 4, 2001, pp. 25-45; and: *Social Marketing* (ed: Michael T. Ewing) Best Business Books, an imprint of The Haworth Press, Inc., 2001, pp. 25-45. Single or multiple copies of this article are available for a fee from The Haworth Document Delivery Service [1-800-HAWORTH, 9:00 a.m. - 5:00 p.m. (EST). E-mail address: getinfo@haworthpressinc.com].

25

be closely associated to the marketer to favorably influence perceptions of the audience. *[Article copies available for a fee from The Haworth Document Delivery Service: 1-800-HAWORTH. E-mail address: <getinfo@haworthpressinc.com> Website: <http://www.HaworthPress.com> © 2001 by The Haworth Press, Inc. All rights reserved.]*

KEYWORDS. Cause related marketing, "Ambush" marketing, field experiment ad study

INTRODUCTION

Corporate philanthropy, where firms donate money and/or services to worthy causes, has evolved into highly publicized "cause-related marketing" (CRM) promotions (Vardarajan and Menon 1988, Barnes 1991). In 1999, these promotions were expected to total over $600 million in the U.S. alone (Gifford 1999), with over 4000 corporations claiming to engage in CRM (File and Prince 1998). Add corporate sponsorships and affinity credit cards, the amount allocated to cause-related appeals increases to several billion dollars (US). Worldwide, this total is expected to dramatically increase as more firms in more countries act on the promised benefits of CRM (Stewart-Allen 1998).

Firms are no longer content with simply giving to charities or social causes hoping for the development of goodwill to assist in future sales. Rather, these companies see tie-ins with social causes as ways to generate immediate sales (Mescon and Tilson 1987; Vardarajan and Menon 1988; Lorge 1998). Although CRM is viewed by some as "self-serving," it does appear to provide companies a way to differentiate themselves from rivals. In an age of parity products and retailers, this is particularly important (Benezra 1996; Dacin and Brown 1997; Bernstein 2000).

A 1996 survey by Cone/Roper found that 76% of those sampled said they would change brands or switch retailers in support of a social cause that was salient to them. This response by potential buyers is up 14% over a previous study conducted by the firm (Cone/Roper 1993). The 1999 Cone/Roper poll reported that 61% of consumers think cause branding should be standard business practice, and 80% felt they have a more positive image of companies who support a cause they care about (Bernstein 2000). However, there is little empirical documentation of the sales or predispositional effectiveness of a CRM appeal. Are buyers more predisposed to believe the CRM sponsor has salient attributes, or to purchase the CRM's products than would be the case with a regular ad commenting on those attributes? Does a closely associated cause work more effectively than a cause not normally associated with the marketer? Does the marketer really need to suggest a financial donation, or can "moral" support noted in the ad work just as well? Are the perceptions of the cause's message affected by whether a corporate sponsor chooses the CRM or "Ambush" cause appeals? Little is known about the cause's success in exposing their message in a compelling way. This study attempts to investigate these issues with a field experiment.

LITERATURE AND HYPOTHESES

Effect on Perceptions

As with most marketing strategies, the ultimate desired outcome of cause-related marketing is to improve sales and profits (Mescon and Tilson 1987; Varadarajan and Menon 1988; Wagner and Thompson 1994). While enhancement of the bottom-line is a primary consideration for firms engaging in cause-related marketing, corporations may also use cause-related marketing programs to create or enhance a favorable image of their product and/or company (Adkins 1999; James 2000). The support of popular causes, or causes which have some relevance to the consuming public, can aid in enhancing the image of the firm through positive association by conveying attributes of social responsibility and public-mindedness (Mescon and Tilson 1987; Stroup et al. 1987; Dacin and Brown 1997).

Cause related marketing can also be used to help counter a negative corporate image. An experiment by Creyer and Ross (1996) found that a hypothetical company was able to minimize the effects of their unethical behaviour (deliberately misleading consumers) by engaging in CRM. Strahilevitz and Myers (1998) showed experimental evidence that CRM can affect feelings of guilt when purchasing luxury or "pleasure-oriented" products, and that this "guilt" may assist in securing support for causes.

Ambush Marketing

Ambush Marketing, like Cause-Related Marketing, associates a corporation with a specific cause or event. However, unlike Cause-Related Marketing, Ambush marketers do not provide financial support to the cause with which they identify themselves. Sandler and Shani (1989) defined the practice as "[A] planned effort (campaign) by an organization to associate themselves indirectly with an event in order to gain at least some of the recognition and benefits that are associated with being an official sponsor" (p. 11).

Sandler and Shani (1989) found that the official sponsors of the 1988 Winter Olympics were correctly identified significantly more often than those companies who engaged in Ambush Marketing. However, this happened for only four of the seven product categories studied. The attempt by the Ambush marketers to reap some of the benefits of association with the Olympics (via broadcast sponsorship and various other unofficial promotional tie-ins) appears to have failed against those four firms who were official sponsors and then vigorously promoted their sponsorship. It should also be noted that the difference in recall and recognition for "Ambushers" did not significantly differ from those firms who were not major advertisers on the Olympic telecast.

While prior research has focused on ambush marketing as a technique used in event sponsorship against a competitor, it is possible for a firm to engage in "ambush" techniques using causal marketing appeals (Geldard and Sinclair 1996). In this manner, Ambush Marketing becomes the practice of providing only verbal support for a cause without a direct financial contribution (although a financial contribution may be implied). Therefore, Ambush Marketing differs from Cause-Related Marketing in that the latter appeal explicitly calls for financial support of a cause in return for consumer purchase of a given product/firm. A recent article (Anonymous 1998) contradicted the Sandler and Shani (1989) results when it reported that whether companies make donations based on consumer's purchases or simply promote the cause without contributing, made no difference to consumers. Even if a firm experienced significantly greater increases in recognition and sales by engaging in cause-related marketing, it has been argued that the extra expense of actual donations to a cause sponsored may not be necessary to get this effect. Not only the ethics and morality of this strategy are subject to question (cf., Meenagan 1994), but negative reactions from suspicious consumers could also backfire with negative perceptions about the "ambusher" (Shoebridge 1997) and the cause. However, there appear to be no published reports of the benefits or penalties to causes from being targeted by an Ambush Marketer.

This literature on perception formation would suggest the proposition that an official CRM sponsor should be more effective in forming favorable beliefs from their ads than the Ambush Marketer. This is because the Ambush Marketer would not be able to claim the CRM appeal in their ads.

H1: A group that receives a social cause-related advertising appeal (financial donation stated), will prompt more positive beliefs about the copy points in the cause ad message than a group who receives an Ambush (no financial stated) version of the ad appeal.

Choice of Causes

Prior to 1954 in the U.S., donations by companies were restricted to those causes/charities that could be shown to be operating in the corporations' or stockholders' interests (Fry, Keim and Meiners 1982). This was a restriction that served to exclude most worthy organizations. With the overturn of this law in 1954, the market was opened for a host of new charities. As cause-related marketing becomes increasingly popular with firms, the choice of causes to support and form an alliance with becomes an important decision (Stewart-Allen 1998; Eastway 1999). The firm has the opportunity to support a cause for which their product(s) is closely related (e.g., Hasbro toys support of Toys for Tots), a cause which supports the image they wish to portray (Proctor and Gamble's sponsorship of the Special Olympics to portray a caring, family-oriented image), or choose a social cause based on its consumer appeal (Varadarajan and Menon 1988, DeNitto 1989; Stewart-Allen 1998). Charitable agencies, groups and social causes have a similar question concerning who to ally with in a causal campaign. While some matches would clearly not fit (e.g., a Tobacco Company and an anti-tobacco group), almost nothing (cf., Eastway 1999) has appeared to guide those on the cause side of the relationship.

To date, there have been no empirically-based studies examining which choice of cause(s) provides the greatest benefit to the firm engaged in cause-related marketing. Some individuals have suggested that a cause linked too closely with the organization would be viewed as self-serving by the buying public, and therefore would work against the firm and the cause sponsored (Anonymous 1998). However, one could also argue that a cause that was clearly associated with the organization would provide easier and quicker recall leading to increased favorable perceptions, purchase and loyalty (Mizerski, Allison and Calvert 1980; Eastway 1999).

H2: A group that receives an ad about a social cause that is closely associated with the sponsor will have significantly more positive beliefs about the ad's copy points than a group who received a cause ad that is not readily associated with the sponsor.

There may also be an effect of the CRM appeal on the audience's perception of the firm or its brands beyond its relationship to the cause. Other beliefs normally associated with product or brand choice may also be enhanced. This process could be explained by the ELM model applied to advertising effects (cf., Petty and Cacioppo 1983). The cause sponsorship would be a positive cue processed with little cognitive effort via the peripheral route to affect and persuasion. Other attitudinal-based paradigms such as the Theory of Planned Behavior (Ajzen 1991; East 1997) could also predict a generalization of affect or perceptions from a CRM appeal.

H3: Groups that receive an ad about a social cause will not differ in their level of beliefs about the cause sponsor's retail oriented attributes than a group who receives a non-cause ad specifically addressing these attributes.

All of the previous proposed effect with the use of a CRM appeal suggest that it is the actual donation to the cause that is important. More specifically, it is the audience's recognition process and belief about it that matters in the process.

H4: Groups that receive an ad about a social cause will have a greater tendency to believe the cause sponsor supports and donates to the cause, than a group that receives a non-cause ad.

Purchase Intentions

A Cone/Roper poll (1997) found that if all else was equal, 76% of individuals surveyed reported they would be likely to switch brands and/or retailers to patronize one who supported a cause they found salient. An earlier poll (1993) reported that 78% of the respondents stated they would be more likely to buy a product associated with a cause they cared about, and 54% would purchase even if the price were higher. If these introspections have any veracity, one can assume that an individual's brand perceptions tend to influence purchase intention. In the case of new users, these perceptions will be strongly influenced by the message(s) to which they are exposed (East 1997).

Firms that provide consumers with a cause associated message may have an advantage over those who provide a straight advertising pitch. For example, Texaco Corporation, sponsors of the Metropolitan Opera for over 50 years, did very little advertising (two minutes) during the broadcast. Analysis of their sales data reportedly showed that many listeners made it a practice to purchase and be loyal to Texaco products because of their financial support of the opera. Texaco's market share among routine listeners was reportedly over two times that of non-listeners (Mescon and Tilson 1987).

While there are many stories about companies experiencing increased sales due to their cause-related marketing, almost all appear to be based on anecdotal evidence, and may be due to simple increased exposure of the brand name. Although several lab experiments have been conducted recently (cf., Dacin and Brown 1997, Strahilevitz and Myers 1998), they used simulated products and samples that included nonusers of the product studied. A controlled test is necessary to determine whether the performance of CRM ads are simply due to general advertising exposure, or because individuals were influenced in their perceptions or intentions to purchase from a company because they sponsored a "worthy" cause. The only field study reported (Strahilevitz and Myers 1998) looked at one part of a multipart study, and used the coupon redemption for two categories of retailers-luxury and utility. No cognitive responses were collected so that other causes cannot be ruled out.

> H5: Groups that receive an ad about a social cause will tend to report a higher intention to purchase from the cause's sponsor than groups who receive a non-cause ad or no ad (control).

METHODOLOGY

Sample, and Determining the Degree of Association for a Cause

The management at a chain of discount liquor stores, and the Head of the Office of Substance Abuse Reduction for a large population (30,000) Southeastern US state university, worked together to increase student awareness of Responsible Alcohol Use at local education institutions. Underage and binge drinking of alcohol is pervasive on college campuses nationwide (cf., Durbin 1999), and was a serious problem on this campus. The early efforts of this group focused on a program using targeted direct mail advertising to reduce underage student purchase and consumption of alcohol.

A program was designed to establish and promote guidelines for new or potential users of alcohol. These guidelines were to provide students an understanding of the maximum level of consumption that would prevent alcohol abuse and its associated problems (e.g., future alcoholism, drunk-driving). Extensive research revealed that the following four usage limits (never drink daily, have only one drink per hour, have a maximum of three drinks per occasion and have a maximum of 12 drinks per week) would provide this "safe" level of "Responsible Alcohol Use."

The university's undergraduate population was targeted for the ads. Undergraduates were viewed as the most important to reach because they were at the period of early use, where lifelong patterns of alcohol use or abuse are often formed (Toner-Schrader and Mizerski 1997).

The University registrar generated a list of classes that had over 40 students enrolled, met at least weekly, and would have students primarily in the 19 to 21 year old range (the national US legal drinking age is 21 years old). From a sample of fourteen classes chosen for the experimental treatments and control, ten instructors allowed their classes to be used in the experiment. Although the classes contained a close representation of academic majors and topics covered in that semester, the final sample of 700 students must be considered a convenience sample.

Choice of a Non-Associated Cause

A second local cause, one that would *not* be readily associated with a liquor store or stores, yet would be equally important to the undergraduate population, was required for the experiment. Pretests, with subjects similar to those used in the main experiment, determined seven important local issues.[1] These issues were then presented to a second pretest group (n = 262) who rated each issue on its relative importance to them. Mean scores ranged from a low of 3.62 for athletic standing to a high of 4.50 for AIDS prevention.

The issue of Campus Night Safety (CNS)[2] was chosen as the not associated cause to use for the liquor retailer. It was rated at approximately the same level of importance by the sample of pretest respondents ($x = 4.30$) as the Responsible Alcohol Use (RAU) issue ($x = 4.16$), while both were rated about in the middle of the seven issues pretested. Another issue, scholarship opportunities ($x = 3.91$), will be used as an example of a bogus cause for later measures. None of the three causes were significantly different (p > .05) from each other in terms of the average importance rating of the pretest sample.

Design and Procedure

Within each class, students were randomly assigned to the control, or one of four treatment groups. The treatment groups each received three exposures of the same ad via direct mail. An address label generated by the registrar was used. The control group subjects did not receive direct mail ads. In addition, one entire class was also included as a control to test if communication within a class could be expected. No differences in control responses were found so the control groups were combined for further analyses.

The ads were on a 5 3/4" × 8 1/2" postcard format. Each treatment subject received one postcard every seven days. Approximately three days following the arrival of the last direct mail ad, students in the sampled classes were asked to fill out a questionnaire by one of the experimenters. This was done in class, and was the first time the students could have become aware of the experimenter, the general nature of the experiment and the chain of liquor stores' possible association with the study.

All of the data was collected within a 36-hour period. Debriefing of the subjects occurred approximately one week after data collection to ensure secrecy during the experiment. Although all subjects were asked to identify the reason for the survey, none of the subjects correctly identified the experiment. Therefore, a demand artifact (cf., Shimp, Hyatt and Snyder 1991) does not appear to be a significant effect in the subjects' responses.

Most of the total sample (n = 459, 65.6% of the total) said they would purchase alcohol within the next two weeks. Twenty-eight (28%) of those were under the age of 21 (the legal drinking age) at the time of data collection. Because intentions to purchase in the next two weeks were elicited, only those who said they would buy will be used to test the hypotheses.

Ad Formats

Four different ad formats were used to test the hypotheses. The four copy points for the Responsible Alcohol Use (RAU) message were preceded by either a financial support (CRM) statement ("a portion of every [liquor store chain name] sale supports [university's] programs for Responsible Alcohol Use"), or a more ambiguous non-financial support (Ambush) statement ("[liquor store chain name] supports [university's] efforts toward promoting Responsible Alcohol Use") in the ad.

Four statements were developed for the Campus Night Safety (CNS) treatment and for a treatment that would provide a commercial retail-oriented message (Ad). The Campus Night Safety and retail-oriented ad only statements were preceded by a financial statement ("A portion of every [liquor store chain name] sales supports [university's] programs for night safety," or "A portion of every [liquor store chain name] sale supports [liquor store chain's] programs for improved operations," respectively). Efforts were taken to make the formats identical in length and complexity, and different only in message content (see Table 1 for each treatment's copy points).

Dependent Measures

Group Identification. The questionnaire was presented by the experimenter as a confidential survey of student opinions concerning alcohol use. No names were elicited for the survey itself although the last four digits of the student's ID number were requested. The students were asked to acknowledge their voluntary consent to the survey by signing their name on a separate document often used in campus experiments. This consent form, along with the last four digits of their ID, was later used to identify the subject, and the experimental group to which s/he belonged. Post-experiment debriefing showed none of the subjects were aware that their responses were identifiable.

Drinking Behavior. Subjects were asked two questions concerning the average number of alcoholic drinks they consumed per occasion, and the frequency of these occasions. These responses provided an often used scale (cf., Toner-Schrader and Mizerski 1997) of drinking behavior (abstainer, light, medium and heavy) that was used as a main effect in the analyses. Previous research had shown that the respondent's drinking behavior was a significant effect on how they perceived responsible drinking messages.

Beliefs About the Liquor Retailer. The subjects were then asked about the likelihood that a competitor of the cause's sponsor, and then the cause's sponsor, has the following attributes: the most store locations, the lowest prices, provides the fastest service and checks age identification closest. Previous company research showed these attributes were salient in customer decision-making. These attributes were claimed in the retail-oriented ad (for the cause's sponsor) treatment only.

Beliefs About the Causes. The subjects were next asked the degree to which they agreed to the four statements used in the ads for the associated (Ambush and CRM Responsible Alcohol Use), and the not-associated (CRM Campus Night Safety) cause ad appeals. A five-point scale, anchored by strongly disagree (1) and strongly agree (5), was used.

Intention to Purchase from a Retailer. The subjects were asked the likelihood they would purchase (". . . the next time you purchase alcohol")[3] from the cause's sponsor, the major competitor in the retail liquor category or from another liquor retailer. This information was used to see if the ad claims generalized to other retailers. The subjects responded to each statement of a copy point on a five-point scale that ran from very unlikely (1) to very likely (5), or they could note that they don't purchase alcohol. No generalization of beliefs to other liquor retailers was found.

Belief About Donation. Each subject was asked the extent to which each of the two major liquor retailers (cause's sponsor and the sponsor's major competitor) donated to a program of Responsible Alcohol Use (RAU), Campus Night Safety (CNS), and student scholarships (bogus cause); as compared to other retailers. They responded to each question on a five-point scale anchored by much less (1) to much more (5).

Covariates. Finally, the students' age, gender, class standing (freshman, etc.), academic major and last 4 digits of their student number were requested. When all of the subjects in a class were finished with the questionnaire, they were shown a card similar to the direct mail pieces sent, with the cause sponsor's name and logo shown as on the treatments ads. They were asked to note on the questionnaire if they remembered receiving one or more cards like the one shown, and if so, what the message said. These responses were later coded to a correct yes/no response that served as a possible covariate of ad recognition. Recognition was not a significant effect on the responses. This may be due to the very high level of correct recognition (over 95%) reported.

RESULTS

Mean treatment and control group responses for each dependent measure are shown in Table 1. The dependent measures provide mean group responses to beliefs about each treatment's four ad copy points,

TABLE 1. Mean Belief and Purchase Intention Responses by Group, for Purchasers of Alcohol in the Next Two Weeks[1]

Dependent Measures	Control N = 177	Ad N = 68	Ambush RAU n = 67	chairman RAU n = 73	chairman CNS n = 74
Retail Ad (Ad) copy points[2]					
* Has Most locations	4.01	4.08	4.05	3.96	4.08
* Has Lowest prices	2.98	3.18	2.92	2.79	2.63
* Has Fastest service	3.49	3.55	3.51	3.33	3.43
* Checks IDs closest	4.11	4.14	4.00	4.06	4.14
Responsible Alcohol Use (RAU) copy points[2]					
* Never drink daily	3.72	3.94	3.86	4.08	3.75
* Only 1 drink/hour	3.00	2.94	3.09	3.14	3.14
* Only 3 drinks /occasion	2.74	2.81	2.85	3.11	2.89
* Only 12 drinks/week	2.57	2.69	2.94	2.79	2.55
Campus Night Safety (CNS) copy points[2]					
* Walk with a friend	4.58	4.59	4.49	4.62	4.72
* Report suspicious	4.28	4.31	4.31	4.25	4.69
* Vary routine	3.87	3.71	3.78	3.84	4.23
* Never hitchhike	4.75	4.82	4.54	4.68	4.82
Extent of donation[3]					
* Responsible alcohol use	3.14	3.18	3.58	3.58	3.43
* Campus Night Safety	2.85	3.00	3.69	2.92	3.42
* Student scholarships	2.54	2.73	2.75	2.67	2.86
Likely to purchase from Liquor Retailer[2]	3.31	3.40	3.22	3.22	3.35

Header spanning: **TREATMENT GROUPS** over Ad, Ambush RAU, chairman RAU, chairman CNS.

[1] n = 459 subjects, but number analysed varies slightly by dependent measure because of missing data.
[2] Responses scaled from "very unlikely" (1) to "very likely" (5)
[3] Subjects were asked, "Compared to other liquor stores, rate the extent to which the causal sponsor donates to [the cause]. Responses were scaled from "much less" (1) to "about equal" (3) to "much more" (5)

the respondents' perceived extent of donation of the sponsor to the social cause, and the respondents' likelihood of purchasing from the cause's sponsor (liquor retailer) in the next two weeks.

The Importance of Stated Financial Commitment

The first hypothesis proposed that a group receiving an ad with a stated financial donation to a cause (a CRM "requirement") would prompt stronger beliefs about the copy points in the advertisement, than an identical ad with no financial commitment noted-or an Ambush cause ad. The most appropriate test of this hypothesis would be to compare the CRM (financial donation tied to sales) and Ambush (financial support not specifically stated) Responsible Alcohol Use (RAU) groups.

The CRM ad showed mean belief scores that were greater than the "Ambush" ad treatment on three of the four copy points (see Table 1). The trend in the mean beliefs is less clear in comparing against the control and two alternative ad treatments (retail-oriented and Campus Night Safety). In order to test for statistical significance, a 5 (treatments and control) group × 4 levels of alcohol use ANCOVA was applied to the data. The respondents' gender, if legal age and major subject area for their undergraduate degree served as potential covariates. None of the four beliefs about the Responsible Alcohol Use copy points were significantly different between the CRM and Ambush appeals. Nor were any of the other treatment groups' (CNS, Ad) or the control group's beliefs on these (RAU) copy points significantly different from the others ($p > .05$). There were main effects of alcohol usage[4] for the "never drink daily" and "only three drinks per occasion" copy points ($p < .001$, $F = 5.56$, 3 df and $p < .01$, $F = 3.82$, 3 df, respectively). Usage and belief were positively associated in both, so heavy users tended to provide stronger beliefs about Responsible Alcohol Use. At least in this experiment, beliefs and behavior about Responsible Alcohol Use may not be associated. There was also a significant effect of the covariate of respondent gender, with women tending to have stronger beliefs about both copy points ($p < .05$), independent of the main effects. However, failure to find a treatment main effect or a treatment interaction meant hypothesis one was not supported. A stated donation tied to sales did not elicit stronger beliefs about Responsible Alcohol Use, the cause's message.

The Importance of the Cause's Association to the Sponsor

The second hypothesis suggested that a group receiving a cause appeal that is closely associated with the product category, would tend to have more positive beliefs about its copy points than a cause that is not associated with the category. To test this hypothesis, one would compare the performance of the two Responsible Alcohol Use ad appeals (CRM and Ambush) against the CRM Campus Night Safety ad treatment. Because the copy points are nested within the treatments (i.e., RAU and CNS copy points are different), direct comparisons are inappropriate. Instead, one could compare the number of beliefs (out of four total) each treatment produced that was significantly larger than the (no ad) control group, against the relative number of beliefs produced by the other treatments against the (no ad) control group. Mean beliefs for each group are shown in Table 1.

The results showed that the closely associated cause, Responsible Alcohol Use (represented by CRM and ambush RAU groups), failed to outperform any of the other treatments or the control group (no ad) in developing beliefs about the four copy points in the two RAU treatments. However, when one looks at the Campus Night Safety (CNS) not-associated cause, the CNS group provided higher mean positive beliefs on three of the four cause copy points. It tied for the highest belief on the fourth copy point.

In order to ascertain whether these mean differences were statistically significant, the respondents' reported belief for each Campus Night Safety copy point was analyzed with a 5 (treatment and control group) × 4 (level of alcohol use) ANCOVA. The results of these analyses show that there was a significant ad treatment effect on three of the four CNS copy points. Only "walk with a friend" failed to show a significant difference in belief by treatment.

For the Campus Night Safety belief about "report suspicious activity," there was a significant main effect of ad treatment ($p \leq .001$, F = 4.60, 4 df) and an interaction of the respondents' reported level of alcohol use and ad treatment ($p \leq .04$, F = 1.84, 12 df). Applying a Tukey HSD test showed that the CRM Campus Night Safety ad[5] prompted significantly stronger beliefs than either of the two RAU groups (CRM and Ambush) only. The significance of the interaction with use of alcohol (positively associated), however, is unclear. Gender was a significant covariate ($p \leq .01$, F = 6.22, 1 df), with women tending to provide a stronger positive belief about that copy point irrespective of the ad treatment they received, or level of alcohol use they reported.

The belief about the Campus Night Safety copy point, "vary your routine," showed main effects of ad treatment ($p \leq .05$, F = 2.31, 4 df) and level of alcohol use.[6] The respondent's gender (women had a higher average belief) and if they were of legal age to purchase (those of legal age tended to have higher average beliefs) were significant covariates. In order to determine which ad treatment groups differed on their belief about the "vary your routine" copy point, a Tukey HSD multiple means test was applied to the data. The CRM Campus Night Safety treatment group had a significantly higher ($p \leq .05$) mean belief than all other treatments and the control. The potential effect of an Ambush ad could not be directly ascertained as no ambush treatment was offered. The lack of a significant effect in the Responsible Alcohol Use ads would tend to suggest no effect would be expected.

Finally, the groups' belief about the Campus Night Safety copy point of "never hitch hike" were analyzed for significant differences. A 5 (treatment and control) $\times$ 4 (levels of alcohol use) ANCOVA was again used. There were significant main effects of both the ad treatment received ($p \leq .05$, $F = 2.35$, 4 df) and the level of alcohol use reported by the respondent. Gender was again a significant covariate.

In order to determine which ad treatments were significantly different in terms of belief about the "never hitchhike" copy point, a Tukey HSD test was used. This analysis showed that the group that received the "Ambush" Responsible Alcohol Use ads had significantly lower beliefs about "never hitchhiking" than all other groups except the CRM Responsible Alcohol Use group. Upon closer inspection, (note the control and ad groups are not different in the Table) it may be that both versions of the Responsible Alcohol Use ads (CRM and Ambush) appeared to lower the audience's beliefs about this copy point. Because the ad did not address it specifically, this finding needs caution and additional supporting evidence for its interpretation.

Looking across these results, it appears that the "not associated" cause, CRM Campus Night Safety, was more effective than the "closely associated" cause (Ambush or CRM Responsible Alcohol Use) in developing positive beliefs about the social message featured. Therefore, the second hypothesis is not supported.

Belief About Retailer Attributes

The hypothesis that the CRM appeals (Responsible Alcohol Use, Campus Night Safety) would do as well as a retail-oriented ad alone (Ad) would need to provide beliefs that were not significantly different between ad treatment groups on the ad copy points. In two of the four copy points, there were no significant effects found. For the copy point, "checks ID closest," there was a main effect of respondents' reported alcohol usage, but no ad treatment effects, nor significant covariates. For the copy point of "lowest prices," the retail-oriented ad treatment group had the most positive belief. This effect of treatment was statistically significant ($p \leq .017$, $F = 3.05$, 4 df), with the Ad group having a significantly more positive belief than all of the other groups. The retail-oriented ad format obtained the highest belief on two out of four total copy points. The messages that featured social cause information did as well as the straight retail-oriented ad appeal on half of the retail-oriented copy points, providing partial support for the third hypothesis.

It should be noted that there were no significant effects of ad treatment for any of the groups beliefs about the liquor chain's main competitor on these retail-oriented copy points. Therefore, the ad treatment effects did not generalize or get misattributed to how the groups viewed the competitor, at least on the copy points measured. The respondents' perception of the cause sponsor's competitor was not significantly influenced by exposure to the sponsor's ad treatments.

Beliefs About the Retailer's Support and Donation

The groups who received the CRM appeals (Responsible Alcohol Use and Campus Night Safety) provided more positive beliefs that the marketer donated to those causes. However, the groups' beliefs about donating to student scholarships, the bogus cause, were not significantly different. The CRM groups did appear to form more positive beliefs than their comparison groups.

Using the same 5×4 ANCOVA used in previous analyses, both treatment ($p \le .002$, $F = 4.19$, 4 df) and alcohol usage main effects were found. Applying a Tukey HSD multiple means test on the data found all three social cause ad treatment groups (Ambush and CRM responsible and CRM Campus Night Safety) were significantly different ($p < .05$) from the retail-oriented ad or control groups. These three social cause ad appeal groups, however, do not significantly differ from one another although the mean scores are generally in line with the hypothesis.

Intention to Purchase

The last hypothesis proposed that the cause sponsor's statement of financial support (CRM), when used on an associated cause (Responsible Alcohol Use for a sponsoring liquor retailer), should prompt those respondents to report significantly stronger mean intention to purchase "the next time" from the cause sponsor. Because the sample contained only those who would purchase in the next two weeks, their intention related to this time period. The mean intention scores of the groups are shown in the table. In order to ascertain if there was any effect of the cause ad treatment on a group, the data was analyzed by a 5 (treatments and control) $\times$ 4 (level of alcohol use) ANCOVA. There were no statistically significant differences found (p > .05). The two cause ads (Responsible Alcohol Use and Campus Night Safety), be they closely associated, Ambush or CRM, had no effect on the subjects' reports of intending to purchase from the sponsoring liquor retailer. No treatment effects were found for the respondents' intention to purchase from the liquor retailer's competitor either. Hypothesis five is not supported.

SUMMARY AND CONCLUSIONS

A field experiment using direct mail ads found that cause-related ad appeals could develop both favorable beliefs about the social marketing message of the cause and be almost as effective as a retail-oriented ad. The sponsoring firm did not have to advertise that financial donations were provided or were linked to sales (i.e., Cause-Related Marketing) to be effective. Although it appeared the audience correctly perceives a CRM as compared to an Ambush appeal, it didn't influence the beliefs about the cause's message or perceptions of the sponsor.

The finding that a marketer did not need to state a financial donation in causal advertising to influence its audience may provide conflicting findings to an earlier work by Sandler and Shani (1989). This supports an earlier report (1998). Although potential consumers appear to recognize and remember a donation, an ambush cause appeal did work as well as a CRM ad for developing some perceptions. The necessity of stating a donation contingent on purchase of the sponsor's products is not supported with this data.

Nor did the cause need to be associated with the sponsor. In this experiment, the most effective social cause appeared to be that of "Campus Night Safety"-not one normally associated with this or any other liquor retailer in the market. Post-tests on the other ad groups and the control group failed to find those respondents naturally expected an association of sponsoring Campus Night Safety and the liquor retailer. The exposures of the direct mail ads were effective on this appeal.

Although beliefs about the social cause, the cause's sponsor, and the perception of the sponsor's commitment to the cause were affected, intention to purchase from the cause's sponsor was not. Perhaps the treatment message, creative execution or level of exposure was inadequate for this task. It is also possible that a stochastic pattern had developed in preference (cf., East 1997) so that the progression from cognitive change to behavior would take substantially more time, if ever

(Ehrenberg 1988). However, the relatively young age and inexperience of the sample (nominally new users) would question that explanation.

Expectations about intentions to purchase should note that a substantial number of the underage future purchasers (28%) in the sample may view intention to purchase as something less than a free choice response. They may feel constrained in their options for actual purchase because of its legal implications and potential punishment. Many may pay others to do the purchasing in the store. Therefore, significantly increasing favorable beliefs about the sponsor reflects a good performance for a social cause appeal with this very limited three-exposure direct mail campaign (James 2000).

LIMITATIONS

Some acknowledged limitations include the low rate of re-exposure and attempt to back this campaign with a total integrated marketing program with in-store exposure, other supporting media and a significantly larger promotion and advertising budget. Single measures for the two constructs of intention to purchase and belief the firm donates to the cause must be viewed with particular caution. Multiple items would tend to increase reliability and validity of the findings and should be explored in future research. External generalization of these findings requires a broader test of causes and their support. Given the range of support possible, other local causes and large national programs may prompt different results. The chosen social causes were also both potentially negative to the audience, so more "uplifting" (e.g., Make-a-Wish Foundation) causes could be better performers. Although both social causes scored well in pre-tests concerning their importance to the respondents, they and many other social causes often portray negative themes. This portrayal of a cause may impose an additional burden to effectiveness.

More empirical work in the field needs to replicate the few lab experiments in the literature. It would also help if there were attempts to tie the early information processing of new users to their ultimate purchase (cf., Strahilevitz and Myers 1998). This would help marketers better understand what aspects of charitable causes are associated with trial purchase behavior, consumer satisfaction and repurchase. More work is needed to evaluate what benefits beyond the financial payoff the cause can receive. Will the cause's image be enhanced for its fundraising and charitable activities? Can the cause's image be damaged through poor sponsor choice or having too many sponsors?

A broader range of cause messages and sponsor types needs to be tested. The brands tested in this field experiment were leaders in their category, liquor retailers. What about new entrants or small brands? Could they derive a disproportionate effect because a CRM appeal would associate them with a well-known cause?

Will family-oriented products like cereals and grocery retailers need causes linked with positive family themes? Future research in the use of Cause-Related Marketing programs and advertising themes will need to address the degree of consistency in the effects across these conditions, and among different audiences targeted.

NOTES

1. Issues included clean environment, AIDS prevention, academic standing, Campus Night Safety (CNS), Responsible Alcohol Use (RAU), scholarship opportunities and athletic standing.

2. A series of brutal assaults on students walking at night immediately before the experiment mobilized the police, the university and the media to ultimately develop a campaign to get students aware of safe behavior when walking at night.

3. Only those subjects (n = 459) who reported they would purchase alcohol in the next two weeks were used throughout the analyses.

4. An alcohol use main effect does not offer a test of any hypotheses, and will not be further discussed.

5. An Ambush version was not tested.

6. Level of alcohol use alone does not provide a test of the hypotheses, and won't be discussed to save space.

REFERENCES

Adkins, Sue (1999), The Wider Benefits of Backing a Good Cause. *Marketing*, (Sept. 2), 20-21.

Anonymous (1998), When Does Cause-Related Marketing Work Best? *Nonprofit World*, (Sep/Oct), 55.

Ajzen, Icek (1991), The Theory of Planned Behavior. In Locke, E.A. (ed.), *Organizational Behavior and Human Decision Processes*, 50, 179-211.

Barnes, Nora Ganim (1991), Joint Venture Marketing: A Strategy for the 1990's. *Health Marketing Quarterly*, 23-36.

Benezra, Karen (1996), Cause and Effects Marketing. *Brandweek* (April 22), 38-40.

Bernstein, Peggy (2000), Philanthrophy, Reputation go Hand in Hand. *PR News*, 56:3, (Jan. 17), 1.

Cone/Roper Study (1993), A Benchmark Survey of Consumer Awareness and Attitudes Towards Cause-related Marketing. Cone Communications, Boston, MA.

Creyer, Elizabeth H. and William T. Ross, Jr. (1996), The Impact of Corporate Behavior on Perceived Product Value. *Marketing Letters*, 7 (2), 173-185.

Dacin, Peter A. and Tom J. Brown (1997), The Company and the Product: Corporate Associations and Consumer Product Responses. *Journal of Marketing*, 61 (Jan), 68-84.

DeNitto, Emily (1989), Marketing with a Conscience. *Marketing Communications*, May, 42-46.

Durbin, Dee-Anne (1999), Colleges Trying Harder to Discourage Excessive Student Drinking. *Nanotines, www.nanotines.com/noframes/story/0,2107,86981-137402-957775-0,00.html*

East, Robert (1997), *Consumer Behaviour: Advances and Applications in Marketing.* Prentice-Hall: London.

Eastway, Jocelyn (1999), The Corporate Conscience. *Business Review Weekly*, (June 4), 84-91.

Ehrenberg, Andrew (1988), *Repeat Buying: Facts, Theories and Applications*, 2nd edition. Oxford University Press: NY.

File, Karen M. and Russ A. Prince (1998), Cause-Related Marketing and Corporate Philanthropy in the Privately Held Enterprise. *Journal of Business Ethics*, 17, 1529-1539.

Fry, Louis W., Gerald D. Keim and Roger E. Meiners (1982), Corporate Contributions: Altruistic or For-Profit? *Academy of Management Journal*, 25:1, 94-106.

Geldard, Edward and Laurel Sinclair (1996), *The Sponsorship Manual: Sponsorship Made Easy.* The Sponsorship Unit, Victoria, Australia.

Gifford, Gayle (1999), Cause-Related Marketing: Ten Rules to Protect Your Nonprofit Assets. *Nonprofit World*, 17:6, Nov/Dec, 13.

James, Dana (2000), For Confectioner, Charitable Acts Make Pot Even Sweeter. *Marketing News*, (June 19), 6-7.

Meenaghan, Tony (1994), Point of View: Ambush Marketing: Immoral or Imaginative Practice? *Journal of Advertising Research*, (September/October), 77-88.

Mescon, Timothy S. and Donn J. Tilson (1987), Corporate Philanthropy: A Strategic Approach to the Bottom-Line. *California Management Review*, 29 (Winter), 49-60.

Mizerski, Richard, Neil Allison and Stephen Calvert (1980), A Controlled Field Study of Corrective Advertising Using Multiple Exposures and a Commercial Medium. *Journal of Marketing Research*, 27:3, 341-348.

Petty, Richard and John Cacioppo (1983), Central and Peripheral Routes to Persuasion: Application to Advertising. In Percy and Woodside (eds.), *Advertising and Consumer Psychology,* Lexington Books: D.C. Heath and Company, 3-24.

Sandler, Dennis M. and David Shani (1989), Olympic Sponsorship vs. "Ambush" Marketing: Who Gets the Gold? *Journal of Advertising Research*, 24 (Aug/Sept), 9-14.

Shimp, T., T. Hyatt and D. Snyder (1991), A Critical Appraisal of Demand Artifacts in Consumer Research. *Journal of Consumer Research*, 18:3, 275-283.

Shoebridge, Neil (1997), Dangerous Games for Outsiders. *Business Review Weekly,* (June 16), 91.

Stewart-Allen, Allyson L. (1998), Europe Ready for Cause-Related Campaigns. *Marketing News,* (Jul 6), 9.

Strahilevitz, Michal and John G. Myers (1998), Donations to Charity as Purchase Incentives: How Well They Work May Depend on What You Are Trying to Sell. *Journal of Consumer Research*, 24 (March), 434-446.

Stroup, Margaret A., Ralph L. Neubert and Jerry W. Anderson, Jr. (1987), Doing Good, Doing Better: Two Views of Social Responsibility. *Business Horizons*, 30 (Mar/Apr), 22-25.

Toner-Schrader, Julie and Richard Mizerski (1997), An Investigation of the Relationship Between Need for Affect and Response to Alcohol Public Service Announcements. *Journal of Non Profit and Public Sector Marketing*, 9:3, 41-72.

Varadarajan, P. Rajan and Anil Menon (1988), Cause-Related Marketing: A Coalignment of Marketing Strategy and Corporate Philanthropy. *Journal of Marketing*, 52 (July), 58-74.

Charitable Donations as Social Exchange or Agapic Action on the Internet: The Case of Hungersite.com

Leyland Pitt
Sharon Keating
Lise Bruwer
Marie Murgolo-Poore
Nigel de Bussy

SUMMARY. Donations to charity have long been of interest to marketing academics seeking to understand the relationships between nonprofit organizations and their customers. A key area of concern is that of motivation-why do individuals donate time, money and other resources to charities in general or to particular charities? While marketers in particular, and social scientists in general, have explained donation and gift giving in terms of the exchange paradigm, more recently consumer researchers have introduced the notion of agapic (or unselfish) behavior to explain some aspects of gift giving. Using the case of a successful charitable Internet site, Hungersite.com, this paper attempts to contrast the exchange and agapic paradigms of donation behavior, with the re-

---

Leyland Pitt, Sharon Keating, Lise Bruwer, Marie Murgolo-Poore, and Nigel de Bussy are affiliated with the School of Marketing, Curtin University of Technology, GPO Box U1987, Perth, 6845, Western Australia (E-mail: *pittl@cbs.curtin.edu.au*).

[Haworth co-indexing entry note]: "Charitable Donations as Social Exchange or Agapic Action on the Internet: The Case of Hungersite.com." Pitt, Leyland et al. Co-published simultaneously in *Journal of Nonprofit & Public Sector Marketing* (Best Business Books, an imprint of The Haworth Press, Inc.) Vol. 9, No. 4, 2001, pp. 47-61; and: *Social Marketing* (ed: Michael T. Ewing) Best Business Books, an imprint of The Haworth Press, Inc., 2001, pp. 47-61. Single or multiple copies of this article are available for a fee from The Haworth Document Delivery Service [1-800-HAWORTH, 9:00 a.m. - 5:00 p.m. (EST). E-mail address: getinfo@haworthpressinc.com].

KEYWORDS. Exchange paradigm, agapic, gift giving, charity, donation behavior

INTRODUCTION

The way in which consumers interact with organizations other than those of profit-seeking business firms has attracted the attention of marketing researchers and practitioners, probably before, and certainly since, the publication of Kotler and Levy's (1969) "broadening" of the marketing concept to include other than for-profit organizations. As a result, both practitioners and academics have become more concerned with issues such as how nonprofit organizations can become more market-driven, how to implement business-type marketing strategies in situations where profit is not the driving motive, how to mobilize the resources of for-profit organizations to a cause (also known as "cause marketing" or "cause-related marketing"), and how better to understand the behavior of the customers and various other stakeholders of these organizations. A key focus of both practical and research interest has been the donation behavior of consumers, for, both researchers and practitioners have reasoned, by doing so, organizations who rely on donations rather than pure sales of products and services for revenue and other resources will best be able to optimize their donation potential.

Donor motivation lies at the heart of our enhanced comprehension of consumer donation behavior-simply, there is a need to better understand why consumers donate resources to a particular charitable organization at a particular time. Until recently most of the explanation of this motivation has centered on the exchange paradigm (simply, consumers donate in order to get something in return). Of late however, an alternative theory of agapic-or "unselfish" giving has emerged as an alternative explanation (Belk and Coon, 1993). It is this contrast, with specific reference to charitable giving and cause marketing on the Internet, which is the focus of our article. We proceed as follows: First, we briefly review some of the research on the application of marketing techniques to charitable donations. Second, we contrast the theories of social exchange with that of agapic giving. Then, the major focus of our paper is a case study of a very successful cause marketing Internet site, Hungersite.com. The case is used to compare the relative explanatory power of the exchange and agapic paradigms with regard to charitable giving. We conclude by attempting to tease out lessons for practitioners and researchers alike with regard to the successful implementation of cause marketing strategies to enhance consumer donation behavior.

DONATIONS TO CHARITY:
THE MARKETING LITERATURE

As alluded to previously, a key area of concern to marketing academics, with regard to charitable donation is that of motivation. As such, isolating attributes that can be used to predict the donation behavior of individuals, or considering the difference between those individuals who donate to charity and those that do not, has been the focus of much of the available literature.

With regard to the demographics of donators, William and Thomas investigated the differences between those individuals who are heavy donors to charities (over 5% of income) and those who are light donors (1986/1987). The following were found to be statistically significant differences between the two groups: the age of the respondents, number of children, whether dividends were an income source, and the number of employed persons in the group. Further, Yavas, Reicken and Parameswaran (1981) indicated that when trying to discriminate between individuals who are donors from individuals who are non-donors, it is more beneficial to use socioeconomic variables than organization-specific attitudes or personality variables.

The motivation of individuals to donate to medical research was investigated by Scott (1988). The following four motives were considered; reciprocity, income, career and self-esteem. Results of this investigation indicated that reciprocity and income were important predictors of giving, as were household assets and age.

Yavas, Reicken and Babakus (1993) found that risk perception, that is, the risk associated with donating money and time to non-profit organizations, had little bearing on the money and time donation behaviors of individuals. However the results indicated that the prediction of donation behavior could be improved by considering both perceived risk in combination with demographic variables. Similar results were found by Reicken, Babakus and Yavas (1994) who concluded, that while risk perception could not entirely explain donation behavior, it does have some effect on an individual's decision to donate.

In addition, it has been found that gender roles affect the amount of money donated by individuals to charitable organizations (Louie and Obermiller, 2000). Specifically, individuals gave lower amounts of money to the same charity, when information about individuals within the charitable organization reinforced a negative stereotype for the gender of the donating individual.

Ellen, Mohr and Webb (2000) examined the manner in which consumers evaluate cause related marketing within a retailing environment; specifically grocer and building supply stores. Attribution theory and the gift giving literature were utilized to determine possible factors. It was found that evaluations by respondents were more positive for causes related to a specific disaster rather than a charity dealing with an ongoing cause. In addition, congruency of the donated product with the retailer's core business was considered. No difference was found within grocery stores.

Of particular interest to this discussion, are the results of a study conducted by Robertson and Bellenger (1978). These researchers found, that the response rate for mail surveys increased when the incentive promised to individuals for returning the questionnaire was a donation to a charitable organization (Robertson and Bellenger, 1978). Lower response rates were achieved, when the same cash reward was offered to the individual personally upon returning the questionnaire, or when no cash incentive was involved.

The factors influencing the donation habits of organizations have also been investigated. Petroshius, Crocker, West, Wu and Wolfe (1993) found that the availability of funds for donation to charity within a company was affected and strongly associated with the company's expected earnings in that year. Results also indicated that with respect to solicitation direct mail was the most preferred method, followed by personal interviews, with the least preferred method being by telephone.

While scales designed to measure consumer attitudes toward donating to charity have yielded mixed results in the past, Webb, Green and Brasher (2000) have made considerable progress within this area by developing and testing scales to measure both consumer attitudes toward the act of helping others and toward charitable organizations (2000). As an alternative, Louie and Obermiller (2000) contend that as social desirability pressures may be obscuring results, peer interpretation research techniques may be needed in order to fully expose the factors that influence the donation behavior of individuals.

A CONTRAST:
SOCIAL EXCHANGE AND AGAPIC GIVING

Social exchange has been at the heart of what most social scientists use to understand human interaction; in short it has been argued that we give in order to receive. Of late in the consumer behavior exchange literature, Belk and Coon (1993) have questioned whether the motivation behind gift giving can always be understood as exchange. If this were the case it would mean that we only ever give in order to receive something in return.

According to Mauss (1925) a renowned anthropologist, reciprocity is the motivation behind gift giving. Within the marketing literature, Kotler and Levy (1969) and Bagozzi (1975) have argued that most human dealings can be understood as a form of market exchange. In Sociology, Homans (1961) has asserted that all human interactions can be understood as a form of social exchange. Further, Zaltman and Sternthal (1975) go so far as to propose that the essence of consumer behavior is essentially exchange.

With economic and social exchange models dominating the literature of gift giving, it stands to reason that all forms of gift giving can be understood through the application of one of these models. Yet, Belk and Coon (1993) found evidence for nonexchange gift giving, providing evidence that gift giving can be something other than a form of exchange. Belk and Coon describe "agapic" or "selfless" giving and assert that it is a necessary addition to the exchange models of gift giving which have dominated the available literature (1993).

We now describe and contrast social exchange and agapic giving, as it is these two models of gift giving which provide possible explanations for understanding the success of Hungersite.com.

SOCIAL EXCHANGE

Both the social exchange and economic theories of gift giving share a commonality, in that, according to both models something is given by an individual in order to receive. In short, exchange is considered fundamental to understanding gift giving. Upon receiving a gift an obligation is felt by the receiver to reciprocate with a gift or alternatively an individual gives to receive something else in return, such as, status, thanks or simply a feeling of well being. The intrinsic difference between these two theories, lies in the value placed upon that which is given and that which is received (Belk and Coon, 1993).

Within the economic model of exchange, the value of that which is exchanged is determined by market value, factors outside those involved in the exchange. In contrast, within the social model of exchange, the value of that which is given and received is symbolic, determined by those involved in the exchange (Belk and Coon, 1993).

Therefore, during those times when the economic model of exchange is in operation, the receiver of a gift desires to reciprocate with a gift of similar financial worth. In comparison the social model of exchange asserts that the receiver of a gift will desire to reciprocate with a gift of similar symbolic worth (Belk and Coon, 1993). While, within the social model of exchange the value of that which is given and received is symbolic, the motivation behind such giving is considered to be egoistic. The model assumes that each individual involved in the exchange is trying to maximize an outcome.

AGAPIC GIVING

Belk and Coon (1993) propose that gift giving can be something other than a form of exchange. They assert that giving can be understood through the application of a model based on the agapic love paradigm. Gifts given within the agapic love paradigm are classified as "pure," that is to say, they are given without an expectation of receiving something in return, and are thus unselfish (Parry, 1986).

Such gifts are also given without considering the cost of the gift, as to consider the cost would imply that the economic model of exchange was in effect (Mills and Clarke, 1982).

It is the sentiment of the gift that is important and this overpowers the "gift's economic worth," further the gift does not bind either the giver or the receiver of the gift (Carrier, 1991). Thus, gifts given within the agapic love paradigm are both unbinding and pure (Belk and Coon, 1993).

We now highlight the main differences between these two models of gift giving. Gifts within the agapic love paradigm are acquired spontaneously. They are acquired when something arises that might please the receiver. In contrast, gifts acquired within the social exchange model are not spontaneous; rather they are acquired as a purposeful act leading towards a goal. As such, the choice of gifts within the agapic model is considered emotional, in contrast with the rational thought characterizing gifts given within the social exchange model (Belk and Coon, 1993).

Within the social exchange model the motivation behind gift giving is considered to be egoistic, with each individual involved in the exchange trying to maximize an outcome. In opposition to this the motivation behind gift giving in accordance with the agapic love paradigm is considered to be altruistic. The individual who is giving the gift does so without considering any benefit that may occur in return (Belk and Coon, 1993).

Therefore, gifts given within the social exchange model are considered to be binding and those within the agapic model non-binding. To summarize, a lack of reciprocal obligation characterizes the agapic model, while the symbolic model of exchange is based on reciprocity (Belk and Coon, 1993).

Within the agapic love paradigm gifts are given without considering the cost of the gift, it is the sentiment of the gift that is important and this overpowers the gift's economic worth. Within the social exchange model, money is relevant but only for symbolic reasons (Belk and Coon, 1993).

In conclusion, Belk and Coon consider that gifts characterized by the economic model of exchange, the social model of exchange and by agapic giving can be understood in the form of a continuum and propose that "it seems likely that symbolic gifts given within the social exchange model lie somewhere between economic exchange commodities and the unbinding pure gifts given within the agapic love paradigm" (pp. 407-408, 1993).

We now describe the case of the Hunger Site and consider the extent to which this Web site is best explained by either the social exchange or agapic model.

CAUSE MARKETING ON THE INTERNET: THE CASE OF HUNGERSITE.COM[1]

Introduction

When a surfer lands on the Hunger Site, he or she is instantly confronted with the message "every three seconds someone dies of hunger and 75% of those are children." Below this information is a map of the world. When a country on this map darkens it represents a death from hunger within that country. What is witnessed is a map of the world upon which various countries are constantly darkening.

Underneath the map the surfer is invited to click through in order to donate free food. All that is required of the surfer is a simple click and the site promises that free food will be donated to children who are starving. This action is costless to the surfer and it is quick and simple.

While this may sound too good to be true, as soon as the surfer clicks, the action is instantly reinforced and the surfer is taken to a screen featuring the sites' sponsors, who pay for the donated food. The surfer is informed that through the simple action of clicking, they have donated 0.8 of a cup of staple food to starving children. In addition, the surfer is thanked for their donation.

On the screen, the banners of the sponsors who pay for the food are clearly visible to the surfer. The surfer is asked to consider clicking on the banners of the sponsors, as it is they who pay for the donated food. The obvious benefits to the sponsors are possible click-throughs to their Web site. The surfer is also informed that by supporting these companies they are ensuring that the service the Hunger Site provides will continue.

A surfer may be tempted to continue clicking under the misconception that he or she will be able to solve all the problems of world hunger by constantly donating food but the surfer is informed that the site counts and permits only one click per person per day. The surfer is thus encouraged to visit the Hunger Site regularly and make a difference. Indeed, it is possible for a surfer to make the Hunger Site the default address on their browser, and so donate every day when they log on to the Internet.

History

The Hunger Site was founded in June of 1999 by John Breen, an Indiana software programmer and the site was the first "click to donate" site on the Internet. John Breen initially thought of using the Internet to support Third World education, but upon inspection of the issues he decided that hunger would be his priority. Breen says, "I remember reading that a big problem with educating some children is that they are so malnourished they can't concentrate."

Since the site was founded it has experienced phenomenal success. On average the site receives approximately 200,000 visits from surfers each day. To date more than 101 million visitors have visited the site and have donated more than 198 million cups of staple food to feed hungry children. The donations of food are distributed to starving people in more than 74 countries by Mercy Corps and America's Second Harvest.

Due to the success of the site, it became difficult for John Breen to manage. He approached GreaterGood.com in 1999 to take over the management of the site and also help manage the growth of the site. The Hunger Site is now owned and operated by GreaterGood.com. GreaterGood.com owns and operates a number of other "click to donate" sites including, The Rainforest Site, The Kids AIDS Site, The Child Survival Site and The Breast Cancer Site.

The success of Hunger Site is also reflected in the numerous awards the site has received, including the 2000 Cool Site of the Year Award, the People's Voice at the 2000 Webby Awards.

The Problems of World Hunger

The problem of world hunger is striking, with approximately 24,000 people dying every day from either hunger or hunger-related causes. Sadly, three-fourths of these deaths consist of children who are under the age of five. Most of the hunger-related deaths highlighted by the media are a result of famine and wars. Yet, these deaths account for just 10% of all hunger deaths. In reality, the majority of deaths are actually caused by chronic malnutrition.

Further, it is estimated that over 100 times more people suffer from malnutrition than die from hunger each year. Prior to death, chronic malnutrition can also cause impaired vision, listlessness, stunted growth and increased susceptibility to disease. Chronic malnutrition impedes the inflicted individual from functioning at even a basic level. Ironically, often only a few resources are required to enable an individual to grow enough food to become self-sufficient. Such resources required include; seeds, tools and access to water.

Agencies Working on World Hunger

There are numerous organizations around the world that do invaluable work in the quest to end world hunger. Such organizations include; Mercy Corps, America's Second Harvest, Bread For The World, AmeriCares Foundation, Catholic Relief Services, Congressional Hunger Center, Freedom From Hunger and CARE. This discussion will however focus on Mercy Corps and America's Second Harvest, as it is through these organizations that the donated food from Hunger Site is distributed.

Within the United States, America's Second Harvest is the largest domestic relief hunger organization, distributing more than one billion pounds of donated food every year. The organization supports approximately 50,000 charities and 94,000 food programs within the United States.

Mercy Corps fights hunger across the globe, helping approximately four million people every year in such countries as the Balkans, Asia, the Middle East, Africa and Central America. It supplies food during emergencies and also tries to find lasting solutions to poverty and oppression within the afflicted countries.

How Does Hunger Site Work?

The homepage of Hungersite.com is simplistic and this works to the site's advantage. When a surfer lands on the site, the brief sentence describing the extent of hunger within the world and the world map, which reinforces this message, are in plain view. The "click to donate" button is also boldly displayed. All other information is unobtrusive.

A simple site index is featured on the left-hand side of the page. Across the top of the page, click-through buttons to other donation sites owned by GreaterGood.com are featured. Further deals offered by sponsors of the donated food are featured but once again these are unobtrusive and it is necessary to scroll across the screen in order to study these effectively. For example, one offer by a sponsor promised a 50-cup donation of food in exchange for a purchase made.

When an individual clicks on the "Donate Free Food" button, the computer server registers the donation and adds the donation to the day's total. The individual is then taken to the "Thank You" page where the names of all the sponsors are displayed. It is these sponsors who pay for the food that will be donated.

The sponsors featured on Hunger Site purchase a place or tile on the "Thank You" page for a specified amount of time. As the Hunger Site counts the number of people who click on the "Donate Free Food" button during this specified time frame, it is possible to bill the sponsor for the amount the donated food will cost.

Specifically, each sponsor pays one-half cent per donation. This half-cent purchases food that upon cooking is equivalent to a quarter cup of food. Therefore, the amount of food that is donated not only depends on the number of clicks the site receives, but also upon the number of organizations who sponsor the site. For example, if there is one sponsor on the site, for each click on the "donate free food" button, a quarter cup of food will be donated. If there are two sponsors on the site, for each click, both donations will combine and a half a cup of food will be donated. Therefore, as the number of sponsors on the site increases so does the amount of food that is donated.

The donated food is then distributed by Mercy Corps and America's Second Harvest. It should be noted that donated food is not split equally between these two organizations. Mercy Corps receives two thirds of the donations in order to fight hunger on an international basis.

Sponsors of the Hunger Site benefit from the possibility of a click-through, from those surfers who click-through from the Hunger Site to a sponsor's site. It should be noted that the click-through rate is three times higher on "click to donate" sites than the rate experienced on Internet sites in general. Those behind the Hunger Site believe that this is because those individuals who frequent the Hunger Site are passionate about the cause and as such want to conduct business with organizations who help further their cause. Those who frequent the Hunger Site are also encouraged to find further sponsors for the site and are made aware of the benefit that increasing the number of sponsors on the site provides.

In addition, those individuals who visit Hunger Site are encouraged to spread the word about the site in order to increase the number of donations. Further, they are encouraged to make the Hunger Site the default address on their browser so that they may easily frequent the site on a daily basis and as such increase the number of donations received.

Banners can also be downloaded from Hunger Site and users are encouraged to link their own Web site to the Hunger Site. In addition, Hunger Site merchandise and merchandise from the sponsors of the site can be purchased on the site. An added feature of these purchases is that they also offer a specified amount of food that will be donated upon completion of the purchase.

CONCLUSION:
THE HUNGER SITE AND DONATION BEHAVIOR-
A QUESTION OF "I GET. . . . OR IT'S GOOD?"

Both the social exchange model and the model based on the agapic love paradigm, when applied to the Hunger Site, provide ways of understanding its success. It is not the purpose of this paper to conclude which theory is more powerful but to show how each model can be used as a tool for understanding donation behaviour.

Theorists advocating the social model of exchange would argue that an individual gives, in this case by donating food, in order to receive. Exchange in this case is fundamental. The worth of what the individual gives is symbolic although it does translate into the monetary value of the free food and the individual would not give if he or she were not going to receive something of equal symbolic worth in exchange (Belk and Coon, 1993). Here, the symbolic gift, which is given, is a "click," a "click" that will lead to the donation of food. The symbolic gift that is given in return is a sense of happiness with respect to their action. The individual gives in order to receive the gift of feeling good.

Within the social model of exchange, the motivation behind giving is considered to be egotistic, the individual within the exchange is trying to maximize the outcome. Rational thought characterizes gift giving within the social exchange model, gifts are given as a purposeful act leading towards a goal. As applied to the case at hand, the individual receives this good feeling at a low cost, simply the time and effort required to click-through.

In Table 1 are selections from letters sent to the Hunger Site in its first two months of operation from individuals and press organizations whose motivations for using the Hunger Site can be explained by the social model of exchange.

In contrast, theorists advocating the model of gift giving based on the agapic love paradigm would assert that the gift given by individuals in this case could be understood as something other than an exchange (Belk and Coon, 1993).

Individuals are in fact giving a "pure" gift, the gift is given without an expectation of receiving something in return and is thus unselfish (Belk and Coon, 1993). The motivation behind the gift is emotional, with individuals giving the gift of free food because it is a worthy cause or simply because it is a good thing to do. A lack of reciprocal obligation characterizes this model (Belk and Coon, 1993). The individual is not giving the gift of free food in order to receive something in return. In fact, a smart surfer could do this mechanically every day with little conscious thought by making the Hunger Site the default site on their browser.

Theorists of this model would advocate that costs to the giver are unimportant. In other words, individuals are not motivated to give the free gift, as there is little cost required to do so, it is the sentiment of the gift that is important.

TABLE 1. Letters Epitomizing Social Exchange

This is the greatest use I have ever seen the Internet used for. Everyone wins. People in need get assistance, corporations get advertising, average everyday people are able to help.

August 7, 1999. The Straits Times (Singapore) -"Go on-line and help feed the world's poor-without spending a single cent. . . . And the net surfer? He gets to do a good deed by just clicking a mouse button each day, with no donations from himself at all. The idea, simple as it is, has worked."

July 21, 1999. Newsweek.com-"Click for hunger. . . . a simple and economical way to make a difference. . . . 'It's amazing,' says [a] spokesperson for the Friends of the WFP, the U.S.-based non-profit that supports the U.N. and other hunger relief organizations. 'The Internet has changed everything and I am anxious to see how this will affect the aid programs.' "

In Table 2 are selections from letters sent to the Hunger Site in its first two months of operation from individuals who use the site in a manner explained by the agapic love paradigm.

It is possible to find evidence for both models of gift giving in relation to the Hunger Site, making it a useful example for understanding perspectives on donation behaviour and cause marketing. The site certainly balances the widely accepted assumption that all forms of gift giving can be understood as an exchange. As such, it offers lessons to researchers, practitioners and marketing students alike.

LIMITATIONS AND RECOMMENDATIONS FOR THE FUTURE RESEARCH

This exploratory paper aimed to compare two competing models of donation behavior-social exchange and agapic giving-with a view to discussing the predictive power of each. This was attempted through a case study approach involving an examination of the Hunger Site website. There are a number of limitations to this approach. First, the inherent constraints of adopting a case study methodology. Any findings may be applicable to the case in question only and may not be generalizable. Second, the case chosen involves a Web site. Even if observations made in relation to the Hunger Site are valid for other Web sites, they may not be generalizable to non-Internet gift giving behav-

TABLE 2. Letters Epitomizing Agapic Giving

Thank you for creating this site. It is rare to find something in this world truly dedicated to helping people.

I'm very happy to donate food and life to someone.

I have never seen anything like your site. It is so matter of fact, respectful of people's dignity, informative and totally "nonaffiliated." In a very weird way it reminds me of the spirit of Mother Teresa. Peace be with you all.

---

ior. Third, the evidence used to examine the applicability of the two models to the Hunger Site is somewhat limited, subjective and qualitative in nature.

Nevertheless, we contend that understanding the motivation for gift giving behavior is of vital importance to organizations in the nonprofit sector. Research that directly compares the agapic and social exchange models is long overdue. Further studies could focus on different Web sites, non-Internet gift giving situations or endeavour to generate data of a more quantitative, generalizable nature.

NOTE

1. Information used in this paper all taken from www.hungersite.com

REFERENCES

Bagozzi, R.P. (1975) Marketing as Exchange. *Journal of Marketing*, 39, (Oct), 32-39.

Belk, R.W., and Coon, G.S. (1993) Gift Giving as Agapic Love: An Alternative to the Exchange Paradigm Based on Dating Experiences. *Journal of Consumer Research*, 20 (Dec), 393-417.

Carrier, J.P. (1991) Gifts in a World of Commodities: The Ideology of the Perfect Gift in American Society. *Social Analysis*, 29, 19-37.

Danko, W.D. and Thomas, S.J. (1986/1987) "Identifying and Reaching the Donation Prone Individual: A Nationwide Assessment. *Journal of Professional Services Marketing*, (Fall/Winter) 2 (1/2), 117-123.

Dawson, S. (1988) Four Motivations for Charitable Giving: Implications for Marketers. *Journal of Health Care Marketing*, (June) 8, 2, 121-136.

Homans, G.C. (1961) *Social Behavior: Its Elementary Forms*. New York: Harcourt, Brace and World.

Judson, M., and Clarke, M.S. (1982) Exchange and Communal Relationships. In *Review of Personality and Social Psychology*, Vol. 3, ed. Ladd Wheeler, Beverly Hills, CA: Sage, 121-144.

Kotler, P., and Levy, S.J. (1969) Broadening the Concept of Marketing. *Journal of Marketing*, 33 (Jan), 10-15.

Louie, T.A., and Obermiller, C. (2000) Gender stereotypes and social-desirability effects on charity donation. *Psychology and Marketing*, (Feb) 17 (2), 121-136.

Parry, J. (1986) The Gift, The Indian Gift and the Indian Gift. *Man*, 21 (September), 453-473.

Petroshius, S.M., Crocker, K.E., West, J.S., Wu, B.T., and Wolfe, T. (1993) Strategies for improving corporate philanthropy toward health care providers. *Journal of Health Care Marketing*, 13, 4 (Winter), 10-19.

Mauss, M. (1925) *The Gift: Form and Functions of Exchange in Archaic Societies*. New York: Norton.

Riecken, G., Babakus, E., and Yavas, U. (1994) Facing resource attraction challenges in the nonprofit sector: A behavioristic approach to fund raising and volunteer recruitment. *Journal of Professional Services Marketing*, 45, 26, 45-71.

Robertson, D.H., and Bellenger, D.N. (1978) A New Method of Increasing Mail Survey Responses: Contributions to Charity. *Journal of Marketing Research*, (Nov) 15, 4, 632-642.

Scholder, P.E., Mohr, L.A., and Webb, D.J. (2000) Charitable programs and the retailer: Do they mix? *Journal of Retailing*, 76, 3 (Fall), 393-496.

Webb, D.J., Green, C.L., and Brashear, T.G. (2000) Development and validation of scales to measure attitudes influencing monetary donations to charitable organizations. *Journal of the Academy of Marketing Science*, 28, 2 (Spring), 299-309.

Yavas, U., Reicken, G. and Babakus, E. (1993) Efficacy of perceived risk as a correlate of reported donation behavior: An empirical analysis. *Journal of the Academy of Marketing Science*, (Winter) 21, 1, 65-71.

Yavas, U., Reicken, G. and Parameswaran, R. (1981) Personality, Organization-Specific Attitude, and Socioeconomic Correlates of Charity Giving Behavior. *Journal of the Academy of Marketing Science*, (Winter) 9, 1, 52-66.

Zaltman, G., and Sternthal, B., eds. (1975) *Broadening the Concept of Consumer Behavior*. Ann Arbor, MI: Association for Consumer Research.

The Dark Side
of Globalization and Liberalization:
Helplessness, Alienation and Ethnocentrism
Among Small Business Owners
and Managers

Albert Caruana
Saviour Chircop

SUMMARY. Globalization and liberalization processes are fostering reactions of helplessness and alienation among many affected communities worldwide. Malta, a small island state, has relied upon a protective system to sustain its industrialization since Independence in the mid-1960s. The changes required by the aforementioned processes appear to threaten gains achieved over the last three decades, resulting in reactions of ethnocentrism. The main aim of this exploratory study is to consider the possibility that anomia or feelings of helplessness and alienation are correlated to ethnocentrism. While ethnocentrism has in the past been examined from a consumer perspective, this study focuses on owners/managers from small firms producing mainly for local consumption. Results indicate a strong correlation between the two constructs and

Albert Caruana and Saviour Chircop are affiliated with the Centre for Communications and Instructional Technology, University of Malta, Msida MSD04, Malta (E-mail: acar@cct.um.edu.mt).
Address correspondence to Albert Caruana at the address above.

[Haworth co-indexing entry note]: "The Dark Side of Globalization and Liberalization: Helplessness, Alienation and Ethnocentrism Among Small Business Owners and Managers." Caruana, Albert and Saviour Chircop. Co-published simultaneously in *Journal of Nonprofit & Public Sector Marketing* (Best Business Books, an imprint of The Haworth Press, Inc.) Vol. 9, No. 4, 2001, pp. 63-74; and: *Social Marketing* (ed: Michael T. Ewing) Best Business Books, an imprint of The Haworth Press, Inc., 2001, pp. 63-74. Single or multiple copies of this article are available for a fee from The Haworth Document Delivery Service [1-800-HAWORTH, 9:00 a.m. - 5:00 p.m. (EST). E-mail address: getinfo@haworthpressinc.com].

show that ethnocentrism is higher among those in the woodworking and printing sectors. Anomia tends to be higher among respondent owners and managers that have been operating in a particular sector for less than ten years. Some preliminary implications for theory and policy development for the Agency responsible for restructuring are considered. *[Article copies available for a fee from The Haworth Document Delivery Service: 1-800-HAWORTH. E-mail address: <getinfo@haworthpressinc.com> Website: <http://www.HaworthPress.com> © 2001 by The Haworth Press, Inc. All rights reserved.]*

KEYWORDS. Globalization, liberalization, helplessness, alienation, anomia, ethnocentrism, Malta, exploratory study

INTRODUCTION

Malta's industrialization, after independence in 1964, has been supported by strong import controls on various products. This situation offered protection to new entities in the industrial and manufacturing sectors. More recently, Malta's acceptance of WTO agreements and its current move toward European Union (EU) membership necessitated a process of relaxation and liberalization. With Malta hoping to join the first expansion of the EU around 2004, the process of liberalization has to be complete in a relatively short time. This process is part and parcel of a wider trend toward globalization.

Faced with such developments different countries have reported a certain ambivalence. Many sectors in society question whether the ensuing change and new reality erode the national character or group identity. This overall concern often manifests itself in local disputes about social mores, language, and identity positions. (For example, France valiantly defends the primacy of its national language, while certain Muslim countries seek refuge in fundamentalist reactions.) Malta is currently dealing with such ambivalence.

At around 400,000, the Maltese market is miniscule and it is no surprise that many of the firms that have developed are small, often employing less than 50 persons. Generally, these firms rely on their captive local market and undertake limited marketing and product development. To facilitate integration into the emerging globalization and liberalization of Malta's market, a government Agency has been set up that seeks to provide consulting and limited financial assistance to firms in the different sectors enabling them to undertake the necessary restructuring.

Faced with the emerging reality requiring local firms to compete with imports that are often less expensive and of a more modern design, many small enterprise owners and managers feel daunted, exasperated and helpless. They vainly argue for the maintenance of the status quo, appealing to "nationalistic" sentiments and to some sense of equity for having invested their money and created employment in the past.

In this instance, cries of "Maltese products first, last and foremost!" is one manifestation of ethnocentrism. This important marketing construct represents the belief held, in this case by owners and managers rather than by consumers and customers, "about the appropriateness, indeed morality, of purchasing foreign made products" (Shimp & Sharma, 1987).

Overwhelmed by these processes of globalization and liberalization which seem to have their own dynamic, one possible reaction is a sense of helplessness and resulting alienation. These personality traits and their effect on ethnocentrism do not appear to have received much attention in the social marketing literature. Helplessness and alienation are themselves manifestations of psychological anomia, better defined as "the breakdown of the individual's sense of attachment to society" (Srole, 1956).

While ethnocentrism is often considered from the perspective of consumers, this exploratory study looks at it from the perspective of owners and managers of small businesses. It investigates the existence of a link between anomia and ethnocentrism and identifies demographic variables of the population that are correlates of ethnocentrism. This study also seeks to suggest actions to the restructuring Agency in its social effort to sustain the survival of the sectors involved.

ANOMIA

Etymologically, anomie comes from the Greek *anomia* and literally means "the absence of law." The word has been variously used. Thus, it represents ruthlessness in Euripides; anarchy and intemperance in Plato; sin and wickedness in the Old Testament; and relatively more recently as a human condition of instability. The latter represents Durkheim's reconceptualization of the construct from the earlier work of a fellow French philosopher, Jean Marie Guyau (Orrú, 1987). Durkheim (1893) was preoccupied with order in society. He high-

lighted the concept of individuality while noting, in his work about sui-
cide, that it is these very individual freedoms that can lead to anomie. In
his theory of anomie, he viewed morality as being of a social nature that
exists externally to the individual and constrains personal behavior. Society is seen as the source of morality and the individual has no choice
but to obey the rules of conduct prescribed by society. Durkheim argues
that "all rules of conduct whose transgressions are sanctioned are moral
rules" and acts left to individual discretion would be by definition outside the realm of morality. Anomie describes any form of deregulation
or lack of cohesion that society may suffer from. Durkheim is critical of
what he considered the ill-conceived cultural objectives of industrial
societies, questioning the prevalent value system and its ability to sustain cohesion. In contrast, later researchers have tended not to question
the basic goals of society, as these were widely accepted. They have
been more concerned with the consolidation of industrial societies.

Two mainstreams of theory on anomie developed in American literature. Robert Merton (1957) emphasized the social-structural aspects of
anomie while Leo Srole (1956) focused on the psychological characteristics of anomia. Merton was not concerned with the anomie that results
from unclear definition of cultural goals but from anomie that arises because of the gap between cultural goals and institutional means. He was
particularly concerned with the characteristics of American society with
its disproportionate emphasis on cultural goals (such as the American
dream, wealth and power) over institutional means. It is the culturally in-
duced pressure to be successful that results in the ensuring anomie and
raises the possibility that certain social groups engage in rule breaking behavior. Merton lists five types of adaptations that can take place: confor-
mity, innovation, ritualism, retreatism and rebellion. Therefore, unlike
Durkheim, the ends are acceptable and it is the adaptation that is the problem. For Durkheim the ends themselves are problematic. As a result
much of the research reported in the American sociology literature has
tended to focus on various types of illegitimacy adjustments.

MacIver (1950) defines psychological anomia (or anomy as he calls it)
as "the breakdown of the individual's sense of attachment to society." Con-
trary to Merton, who argues that anomie arises exclusively from capitalis-
tic competitiveness where "those who having lost their ethical goals . . .
transfer this drive into extrinsic values to the pursuit of means instead of . . .
ends, and particularly to the pursuit of power," MacIver (1950) highlights
two additional aspects. First, the issue of culture clash represented by
"those who having lost . . . any system of value . . . having lost the com-
pass that points their course into the future, abandon themselves to the

present." Secondly, rapid social change represented by "those who have lost the ground on which they stood, the ground of their former values." Srole's (1956) psychological theory of anomia builds on the work of MacIver but focuses on the individual level. To distinguish anomie at the psychological level from that at the sociological level, Srole used the term anomia. He identifies five dimensions of anomia that he operationalized into a five-item scale. At a macro level, Srole's theory of anomia looks at social integration. Anomia describes the individual's loss of values coupled with rapid social change that result in a person's lack of integration in modern social life. It is this view of anomia that is adopted in this study. At the micro level, the scale he developed seeks to determine the individual's level of integration with the social system.

Srole's scale is the most widely-used measure of anomia in the social sciences. Srole improved the original five-item scale with the addition of a further four items (cf., Robinson and Shaver, 1973). The resultant nine-item instrument was adopted in 1973 and in subsequent years for use in the annual General Social Survey of the U.S. National Opinion Research Center. Dodder and Astle (1980) made use of the data from the 1973, 1974 and 1976 national surveys generating a total sample of 4487 respondents. Poresky, Atilano, and Hawkins (1981) use longitudinal data among a sample of 58 rural women to compare the internal stability of the Srole scale with the enlarged 9-item scale. Three-year test-retest correlations obtained for both instruments were 0.45 and 0.56, respectively, indicating higher reliability and stability for the 9-item scale. Perhaps more important are Dodder and Astle's (1980) findings that the nine-item anomia scale provides stronger correlations with "virtually every variable" grouped under the three headings of Demographics, Satisfaction and Social Involvements; headings that together make up 31 variables that are traditionally associated with anomia. For example, those with higher levels of occupational prestige, higher levels of education, higher levels of income and more satisfactory finances are associated with less anomia. On the other hand, dogmatism, which refers to the degree of flexibility of values, has been identified as an antecedent variable and results in higher levels of anomia.

ETHNOCENTRISM

Ethnocentrism is a sociological concept first introduced by Sumner (1906) that refers to a tendency to regard the beliefs, standards, and code of behaviour of one's own as superior to those found in other societies. Ethnocentrism often serves the socially useful function of encouraging cohesion and solidarity among group members, but can also contribute to attitudes of superiority, intolerance, and even contempt for those with different customs and lifeways (Levine & Campbell 1972; Wagley 1993, Booth 1979; Worchel & Cooper 1979). Shimp and Sharma (1987) define ethnocentrism as "the beliefs held by consumers about the appropriateness, indeed morality, of purchasing foreign made products." These authors developed an instrument, termed the CETSCALE (Consumers' Ethnocentric Tendencies) which sought to measure consumer disposition in purchasing American-made products versus those of other countries. Ethnocentrism has been found to correlate with a number of demographic variables. The effect of gender on made-in label is mixed. Schooler (1971) and Dornoff, Tankertsley and White (1974) report that women have a more favourable evaluation of products coming from abroad than men, while other studies find no effect (Anderson & Cunningham 1972). Shimp and Sharma (1987) find that in their Carolinas study, the effect of age varies by social class and only older working class individuals manifest ethnocentric tendencies. Min Han (1988), who carried out work in the US, reports that patriotic intensity has a statistically significant relationship with age and sex. Ethnocentrism has also been linked to personality traits that include variables such as innovativeness, dogmatism, risk taking, and inner-outer directedness. For example, in a US study, those exhibiting less dogmatism, which refers to the degree of flexibility of values, have been found to display a more favourable attitude towards foreign products (Anderson & Cunningham 1972). Shimp and Sharma (1987) report a statistically significant correlation of 0.40 between ethnocentrism and dogmatism in their "crafted with pride" study. The link between ethnocentrism and anomia does not appear to have received attention.

METHODOLOGY

To investigate the link between anomia and ethnocentrism, the 9-item Srole scale and the 17-item CETSCALE were used. Each item was measured using 7-point scales anchored 1 = "Strongly Disagree" and 7 = "Strongly Agree." Other classificatory and demographic data consisted of type of business, number of years in the business, whether the respondent was a manager or owner, the number of employees, age and gender. The final instrument consisted of 32 items. Data was collected during 2000 from a convenience sample consisting of individuals attending courses targeting small firm owners and managers. Potential respondents were assured of complete anonymity and that all results would be aggregated. A total of 96 valid replies were obtained. Given the exploratory nature of the study, the reply rate was deemed adequate.

ANALYSIS

The mean and standard deviations of the items in the Srole and CET scales are shown in the Appendix. In terms of demographics and other classificatory variables, 81% were male and 52.1% of respondents were owners. The mean age was 36.70 (sd = 8.38), the number of years with the firm was 13.54 (sd = 9.89) and the average number of employees was 15.93 (sd = 17.40). The internal reliability and validity of the instrument was tested. Reliability tests showed that item-to-total correlations exceeded the 0.35 level in the case of the Srole's scale and the 0.5 level in the case of the CETSCALE. The only exception was the first item in the Srole scale that provided an item to total correlation of 0.29. However, given the extensive testing done with this instrument in previous studies, it was decided to keep this item. The overall coefficient alpha (Cronbach, 1951) for each of ethnocentrism and anomie provided values of 0.83 and 0.96, respectively. These comfortably exceeded the 0.7 threshold and are therefore acceptable (Nunnally, 1978). Principal components factor analysis followed by a varimax rotation was undertaken concurrently on the two scales to determine the dimensionality of the scale as well as its discriminant validity. The first item on the Srole scale provides an ambiguous loading. However, the results shown in Table 1 confirm a clear factor structure with each of the two constructs loading separately.

The sum of the scales for ethnocentrism and anomia were computed. These were used in a 2-tailed correlation analysis to determine whether a link existed between the two constructs. Results show a strong correlation: $r = 0.51$ (p < 0.001). Each construct was investigated with the classificatory and demographic variables collected. T-tests of means on the basis of whether the respondent was a manager or the owner, by gender, by number of firm employees and by respondent age, indicated no statistically significant differences in means. However a split of respondents by type of industry shows higher levels of ethnocentrism in the furniture and printing sectors, while in terms of levels of anomia there is no statistical difference between the two samples (Table 2A). A

TABLE 1. Results of Principal Component Analysis with Varimax Rotation

Question	Ethnocentrism	Anomia
Q1	.693	.376
Q2	.579	
Q3	.739	
Q4	.609	
Q5	.758	
Q6	.776	
Q7	.801	
Q8	.777	
Q9	.710	
Q10	.650	
Q11	.850	
Q12	.608	
Q13	.676	
Q14	.732	
Q15	.659	
Q16	.694	
Q17	.711	
Q18	.332	.462
Q19		.709
Q20	.366	.596
Q21		.634
Q22		.645
Q23		.541
Q24		.611
Q25		.785
Q26		.735

Values less than 0.35 not shown

split of respondents by the number of years they have been with an industry shows that while there is no difference in terms of ethnocentrism, respondents who have been in an industry for 10 years or less exhibit higher levels of anomia (Table 2B).

DISCUSSION

The main objective of this study was to undertake an exploratory investigation of the possible existence of a link between anomia and ethnocentrism among small enterprise owners and managers facing the inevitability of restructuring. The main academic contribution is the

TABLE 2A. Differences in Means for Anomia and Ethnocentrism by Type of Industry

	Type	N	Mean	Std. Deviation	Std. Error Mean	t	Sig
Anomia	Furniture/printing	44	41.43	8.66	1.31		
	Others	52	37.87	12.00	1.66	1.69	.095
Ethnocentrism	Furniture/printing	44	59.85	21.38	3.22		
	Others	52	48.23	22.53	3.13	2.58	.012

TABLE 2B. Differences in Means for Anomia and Ethnocentrism by Years Operating in Industry

	Type	N	Mean	Std. Deviation	Std. Error Mean	t	Sig
Anomia	10 and less	46	42.02	10.25	1.51		
	More than 10	46	36.46	10.36	1.53	2.59	.01
Ethnocentrism	10 years and less	46	52.38	23.81	3.51	−.23	.82
	More than 10 years	46	53.49	22.12	3.26		

support provided for this link among the owners/managers. Clearly further replication is required.

The research also sheds some light on the situation prevailing among small local firms. It shows that these exhibit levels of anomia and ethnocentrism. The level of anomia is even higher among those that have been with an industry for 10 years or less, as they sense the possibility that the prospects of the career they may have invested in could be about to disappear. On the other hand, levels of ethnocentrism are found to be higher among respondents from the printing and woodworking industry. These two sectors are likely to be quite severely hit by the policy of globalization and liberalization and this may account for the higher levels of ethnocentrism reported.

The mean score for ethnocentrism among respondents from small enterprise at 53.55 (sd = 22.66) appears to be lower than the 56.80 mean (sd = 26.95) reported from a study carried out among general households in Malta during 1995 (Caruana & Magri, 1996). Although there is a lapse of four years between the two studies, current scores for ethnocentrism among owners/managers are not that high. They indicate that most are willing to accept the new challenges. Ethnocentrism needs to be weakened if resistance to change is to be surmounted. Overcoming anomia is one way to achieve this aim.

In terms of policy implications, the public sector restructuring agency that has been set up needs to undertake significant marketing activities and show itself to have a practical strategic vision in each sector that it supports. It needs to communicate and promote this direction in a way that is both persuasive and convincing to the owners/managers in the sectors being targeted. While addressing the concerns of the owners/managers, the agency needs to illustrate how threatening circumstances can be a challenge for planned change that could still put the owners/managers on top of things. The use of success stories could go a long way in counteracting feelings of helplessness. There is a clear need for promptness and responsiveness to requests, irrational as they may sound. Often these concerns mask underlying feelings of helplessness and alienation.

As in any study, this investigation has its limitations. Salient among these is that a convenience sample made up of volunteer participants at a strategy course open to all sectors being supported by the agency is used. This may not be completely representative of all small firm owners/managers. Furthermore, the study only considers two constructs that are likely to be part of a wider picture. Finally, while the reported findings for this study provide support for the reliability and validity of the instruments used, the issue of cross-national invariance of the scales has been assumed. The literature supports the invariance of the CETSCALE (Steenkamp & Baumgartner, 1998) but this aspect does not appear to have been investigated in the case of the anomia scale.

The study establishes a correlation between the two constructs. Anomia is likely to be an important antecedent to ethnocentrism. Further replication among similar populations in different countries is required to establish that anomia is indeed an antecedent. More importantly, is the link between the two constructs direct or via moderating or mediating variables? For example, it is known that dogmatism has a direct effect on both anomia (Dodder & Astle, 1980) and ethnocentrism (Shimp & Sharma, 1987). How would this and other constructs fit into the model?

REFERENCES

Anderson, W. T., & Cunningham, W. H. (1972). Gauging foreign product promotion. *Journal of Advertising Research, 12* (1), 29-34.

Booth, K. (1979). *Strategy and Ethnocentrism.* London: Croom Helm.

Caruana, A., & Magri, E. (1996). The effects of dogmatism and social class on consumer ethnocentrism in Malta. *Marketing Intelligence & Planning, 14* (4), 39-44.

Cronbach, L. J. (1951). Coefficient alpha and the internal structure of tests. *Psychometrika, 16* (3), 297-333.

Dodder, R. A., & Astle, D. J. (1980). A methodological analysis of Srole's nine-item anomia scale. *Multivariate Behavior Research, 15,* 329-334.

Dornoff, R. J., Tankertsley, C. B. & White, G. P. (1974). Consumers' perceptions of imports. *Arkon Business and Economic Review, 5* (Summer), 26-29.

Durkheim, E. (1933). *The Division of Labor.* (J. Spaulding, & G. Simpson, Trans.). New York: Free Press. (Original work published 1893).

Levine, R., & Campbell, D. T. (1972). *Ethnocentrism: Theories of conflict, ethnic attitudes, and group behaviour.* New York: John Wiley.

MacIver, R. M. (1950). *The ramparts we guard.* New York: Macmillan.

Merton, R. K. (1957). Social structure and anomie. *American Sociological Review, 3* (June), 672-682.

Min Han, C. (1988). The role of consumer patriotism in the choice of domestic versus foreign products. *Journal of Advertising Research, 28* (Jun-July), 25-32.

Nunnally, J. C. (1978). *Psychometric theory* (2nd ed.). New York: McGraw Hill.

Orrù, M. (1987). *Anomie.* Winchester, MA: Allen & Unwin Inc.

Poresky, R. H., Atilano, R. B., & Hawkins, K. (1981). Anomia in rural women: A longitudinal comparison of two measures. *Psychological Reports, 49,* 480-482.

Robinson, J. P., & Shaver, P. R. (1973). *Measures of social psychological attitudes.* Ann Arbor, MI: University of Michigan, Survey Research Center.

Schooler, R. D. (1971). Bias phenomena attendant to the marketing of foreign goods in the US. *Journal of International Business Studies,* Spring, 71-80.

Shimp, T. A., & Sharma, S. (1987). Consumer ethnocentrism validation of the CETSCALE construction and validation of the CETSCALE. *Journal of Marketing Research, VVIV,* (August), 280-289.

Steenkamp, J. B., & Baumgartner, H. (1998). Assessing measurement invariance in cross national consumer research. *Journal of Consumer Research, 25* (June), 78-90.

Srole, L. (1956). Social integration and certain corollaries: An exploratory study. *American Social Review, 21* (December), 709-716.

Sumner, G. A. (1906). *Folkways.* New York: Ginn Custom Pub.

Wagley, C. (1993). *Ethnocentrism.* Grolier Pub.

Worchel, S., & Cooper, J. (1979). *Understanding social psychology.* Homewood, IL: Dorsey Press.

APPENDIX
Items and Descriptive Statistics

		Mean	Std Dev
1.	Most public officials (people in public office) are not really interested in the problems of the average man	5.23	1.70
2.	Nowadays a person has to live pretty much for today and let tomorrow take care of itself	3.75	1.89
3.	In spite of what some people say, the lot of the average person is getting worse, not better	4.50	1.75
4.	It's hardly fair to bring children into the world the way things look for the future	3.77	1.93
5.	These days a person doesn't really know whom he (or she) can count on	4.88	1.64
6.	Most people really don't care what happens to others	4.65	1.70
7.	Next to health, money is the most important thing in life	4.10	1.96
8.	You sometimes can't help wondering whether anything is worthwhile	4.29	1.80
9.	To make money there are no right and wrong ways anymore, only easy and hard ways	4.33	1.97
	Anomia	**39.50**	**10.70**
10.	Maltese people should always buy Maltese-made products instead of imports	3.48	1.84
11.	Only those products that are unavailable in Malta should be imported	2.94	1.85
12.	Buy Maltese-made products. Keep Malta working	4.54	2.00
13.	Maltese products first, last and foremost	3.32	1.79
14.	Purchasing foreign made products is un-Maltese	2.48	1.47
15.	It is not right to purchase foreign products, because it puts Malteses out of jobs	2.85	1.78
16.	A real Maltese should always buy Malta made products	3.02	1.75
17.	We should purchase products manufactured in Malta instead of letting other countries get rich off us	3.47	1.89
18.	It is always best to purchase Maltese made products	3.72	2.04
19.	There should be very little trading or purchasing of goods from other countries unless out of necessity	2.81	1.76
20.	The Maltese should not buy foreign products, because this hurts Maltese business and causes unemployment	3.06	1.72
21.	Curbs should be put on all imports	2.80	1.82
22.	It may cost me in the long-run but I prefer to support Maltese products	4.04	1.79
23.	Foreigners should not be allowed to put their products on our markets	2.75	1.96
24.	Foreign products should be taxed heavily to reduce entry into Malta	2.88	1.87
25.	We should buy from foreign countries only those products that we cannot obtain within our own country	2.71	1.49
26.	Maltese consumers who purchase products made in other countries are responsible for putting their fellow Maltese out of work	2.68	1.78
	Ethnocentrism	**53.55**	**22.66**

The Impact of Social Marketing
on Social Engineering
in Economic Restructuring

Lance McMahon

SUMMARY. Social Marketing is a rapidly growing marketing sub-discipline based on the premise that bringing successful commercial marketing technologies to bear on problems of individual and social welfare can generate positive outcomes. This paper gives an overview of recent developments in Social Marketing in a global context and discusses the relationship of these developments to those in commercial, not-for-profit or third sector and public sector marketing, and public relations. The paper then relates the global context back to developments in Australasian and Asian nations, with particular reference to social engineering during economic restructuring. *[Article copies available for a fee from The Haworth Document Delivery Service: 1-800-HAWORTH. E-mail address: <getinfo@ haworthpressinc.com> Website: <http://www.HaworthPress.com> © 2001 by The Haworth Press, Inc. All rights reserved.]*

KEYWORDS. Social Marketing, welfare, not-for-profit marketing, third sector marketing, public sector marketing, public relations, social engineering, economic restructuring

Lance McMahon, MSc, is affiliated with the Institute for Sustainability and Technology Policy, Murdoch University, Perth, Western Australia and is Principal of Policy Resolutions.

Address correspondence to Lance McMahon, Policy Resolutions, 48 Sunbury Road, Victoria Park, WA, 6100, Australia (E-mail: mcmahonl@bigpond.com).

[Haworth co-indexing entry note]: "The Impact of Social Marketing on Social Engineering in Economic Restructuring." McMahon, Lance. Co-published simultaneously in *Journal of Nonprofit & Public Sector Marketing* (Best Business Books, an imprint of The Haworth Press, Inc.) Vol. 9, No. 4, 2001, pp. 75-84; and: *Social Marketing* (ed: Michael T. Ewing) Best Business Books, an imprint of The Haworth Press, Inc., 2001, pp. 75-84. Single or multiple copies of this article are available for a fee from The Haworth Document Delivery Service [1-800-HAWORTH, 9:00 a.m. - 5:00 p.m. (EST). E-mail address: getinfo@haworthpressinc.com].

INTRODUCTION:
DEFINING THE TERMS

Social Marketing (hereafter SM) is a rapidly emerging sub-discipline of the Marketing discipline that is growing in influence and interest. Marketing itself grew and diversified as a discipline through the 20th century. Marketing was first taught as a business subject at University of Wisconsin in 1902 (Bartels, 1962), with a narrow focus on sales, and then broadened to being seen as a central and essential "whole of organization" management discipline (Drucker, 1954). Marketing then further expanded to be a broad "whole of society" discipline based on a general understanding of facilitating and consummating exchanges (Kotler and Levy, 1969; Kotler, 1972). The Marketing focus widened from the private market sector, which should be noted as still the central concern, to the public sector and not-for-profit or third sector.

Social Marketing

The term "social marketing" first emerged in the Marketing discipline in 1971 through the agency of Kotler and Zaltman's (1971) seminal article, "Social Marketing: An Approach to Planned Social Change." Andreasen (1995) has provided a formal definition that echoes those of other leaders in the sub-discipline (for example, Kotler and Roberto, 1989 and Goldberg, Fishbein and Middlestadt, 1997):

> Social marketing is the application of commercial marketing technologies to the analysis, planning, execution, and evaluation of programs designed to influence the voluntary behavior of target audiences in order to improve their personal welfare and that of their society. (Andreasen, 1995, p. 7)

SM is part of a larger, non-private market sector marketing concern which include public sector marketing, government marketing, political marketing, not-for-profit marketing, non-government-organization (NGO) marketing, charitable marketing, cause-related marketing and voluntary or "third sector" marketing. While the distinction between SM and commercial private sector marketing is easily made, the distinction between SM and its cousin non-private sector sub-disciplines is not easily made and they have many intersections and overlapping jurisdictions.

It should also be noted that SM can be and often is undertaken as part of commercial private sector campaigns where a company seeks to play a good corporate citizen role. Examples include a company co-branding (for discussion on SM co-branding see Peachment et al. 1999) with a charity where a set percentage of proceeds from commercial sales go to a charitable cause or a company undertaking charitable work under its own auspices, for example, providing a facility for children suffering from cancer. A kindred area of co-branding is Green Marketing, which also seeks broad social outcomes through improved environmental standards (Wasik, 1996).

Social Engineering

Social Engineering (hereafter SE) is a term for the planned and directed process of social change undertaken by the agency of government. SE is effectively the state-based equivalent of commercial private sector marketing. Where the latter attempts to influence behavior to alter consumption of private goods, the former seeks to influence behavior to alter the consumption of public goods or individual relations to society. SE has its roots in the social and behavioral psychology pioneered by Thorndike (1905), Skinner (1948) and Bandura (1969) and the 20th century conviction that social problems would have achievable scientifically-based solutions. However, the 20th century also exposed the sinister side and limitations of SE in the failed large-scale programs of totalitarian social control of Soviet Russia, Nazi Germany and Maoist China.

SE in general faced strident criticisms as a result of the link to totalitarianism, most notably from Popper (1957) and the "Austrian" and "Chicago" schools of economists and philosophers who came to be the influential "new right." Continued criticisms and suspicion of SE center on the role of the state versus the role of the market question. While hardline free marketeers argue that governments should never pursue SE and civil libertarians seek to contain and constrain SE (over concerns about state intrusion and control through "political correctness" or "nanny statism"), most concede that some SE programs are a proper or even essential role for government.

Faced with social problems ranging from the spread of AIDS and other infectious diseases, harmful and unhealthy behaviors such as smoking and other drug use, rises in crime and other anti-social behaviors, governments seek to engineer social changes. Governments also seek to engineer favorable human resource outcomes for the economy, with a productive and skilled workforce providing overall economic benefits and individual welfare benefits.

Economic Restructuring

Economic Restructuring (hereafter ER) is a global phenomenon that has been a notable economic feature since the rise of the modern trading state and the industrial revolution. Since the late 20th century, the exigencies of the increased globalization of markets have led to a greater emphasis and effort by nation states in ER. Large and powerful economic entities such as the United States and the European Union have had to pursue ER in the face of a global competition. The once robust economy of Japan, long held as an economic model, is now suffering a prolonged and intensifying crisis due to a failure to pursue effective ER.

The smaller, isolated developed economies, such as those of Australia and New Zealand, are struggling with the demands of ER. Third World economies such as those of India and sub-Saharan Africa are finding the resources and policy co-ordination required for achieving effective ER elusive, as are the post-communist nations of Central and Eastern Europe. In the wake of the 1997 crisis of capital markets, the "tiger" developing, newly industrializing (NIC) economies of Asia have placed increased emphasis on ER to both neutralize the effects of the crisis and also to regain the previous economic momentum toward development.

Public Relations

Public Relations (hereafter PR) is an element of the marketing communications mix which, like SM, has developed as a distinct sub-discipline of Marketing. PR also has antecedents in management and journalism and retains a practical characteristic of "putting out our story" (Broom and Dozier, 1990, p. 4) or generating a favorable image for an organization both externally and internally. However, as Broom and Dozier (1990), Jenkins (1988), Kotler (1992) and others point out, PR is concerned with establishing and maintaining an understanding between an organization and its publics. Cuitlip, Center and Broom (1985, p. 4) offer a formal definition:

> Public Relations is the management function that identifies, establishes and maintains mutually beneficial relationships between an

organization and the various publics on whom its success or failure depends.

Faced with challenges of ER, PR and SM overlap as elements of a SE response on the part of governments. As such, both PR and SM are essential components of the public policy toolkit.

SOCIAL MARKETING, SOCIAL ENGINEERING AND ECONOMIC RESTRUCTURING

The relationships between SM, SE and ER are multifaceted and vary greatly across jurisdictions. However, one constant is that governments are locked into pursuing ER due to pressures stemming from the increasing globalization of markets. SE is essential to the pursuit of ER as nation states seek to develop their human capital to accept and be better equipped to deal with the pressures of globalization. It has long been accepted that the education, health, welfare and morale of national populations is a key factor in achieving success in the knowledge intensive industries of the "new economy," where competition between nations for a share of global markets and investment is intense.

Previously SE had a "top-down" character. This was obviously so in totalitarian regimes where the use and abuse of state force was applied as a means to secure the SE ends, as regrettably is still the case in the world's remaining totalitarian regimes. However the "top-down" model for SE also prevailed in liberal democracies where governments sought to coerce SE outcomes from citizens. The results of coerced SE were limited due to citizen resistance not so much to the ends but rather to the means applied.

The reasons for citizen resistance to coerced SE are varied and imbedded in national cultures and societies. In general, however, there is an inbuilt tension between the logic of liberal democracy and citizen sovereignty and freedom and coerced SE. This tension is the central concern of Popper (1957) and other leading critics of SE who saw coercion as an erosion of core liberties and a drift towards the SE based totalitarian regimes they were especially critical of. SE represented the "road to serfdom."

As the collapse of the totalitarian regimes of Central and Eastern Europe in 1989-91 showed, even SE backed by abusive state power faced citizen resistance. The rejection of "top-down" models, which had prevailed almost exclusively throughout human history, can be explained in part by the new economic conditions that emerged on a global scale in the 20th century.

The rise of mass consumer capitalism and the attendant symbiotic relationship between consumer and producer challenged the "top-down" model. The development of marketing as a discipline and practice was in itself recognition that consumers could not be told how to behave in a "top-down" way but rather have to be listened to and understood in a "bottom-up" way (Sheth, 1974, pp. 89-114). The way consumers behave had become a complex area for inquiry and the old maxim "the customer is always right" gained new credence.

The new customer- and service-based emphasis in the competitive commercial private sector has a relationship to changes in expectations in the public sector. Citizens accustomed to "bottom-up" models in the private sector expected similar approaches from the public sector and much of the broad management and organizational revolution in the public sector in the last quarter of the 20th century reflects these new expectations and demands.

As citizens expect to be "listened to" by governments and persuaded rather coerced, so SE has had to adopt marketing methods to achieve success. It is as a means to this end that SM and PR have been deployed. In general, PR has played a supporting role to SM in much the same way that PR has contributed to the marketing communications mix for private sector commercial marketing. Much PR practice relates to SM, the key features of which and relationship to ER are set out below. PR in SM is especially important as a link between government agencies and government in general and segments of or the whole of the public.

Following from Andreasen's (1995) definition, SM is concerned with the development of programs to influence citizens to support social ideas promulgated by government. The SE outcomes of SM can be divided into three:

- SM as a means to trigger a one-off, isolated or periodic behavior in citizens such as donating funds to support improvements at a public hospital or volunteering to participate in a day for cleaning up public spaces.
- SM as a means to trigger lasting behavioural change such as quitting cigarette smoking or driving safely.
- SM as a means to trigger change in beliefs and attitudes such as encouraging family planning and countering racism and inter-ethnic tensions.

Even where governments retain and actively deploy coercive powers, in areas such as road safety or use of illegal drugs, SM is used as a means to persuade citizen compliance. In part the logic for this is that voluntary compliance adheres to the maxim of "prevention is better than cure" and uses fewer resources whereas the "cure" of detection and punishment is resource-intensive and less effective. It is certain that SM campaigns have broader reach than coercion in that the experience in many nations is that such campaigns can reach most of a target population whereas coercion will apply only to a very small minority.

SM is also used by governments in campaigns to reinforce broad values essential to the maintenance, social cohesion and prosperity of the nation-state. SM campaigns to encourage intangible beliefs and values such as patriotism, pride and loyalty to the nation-state are universal. SM campaigns are also used to promote and bolster support for particular national systems of governance, for example, the marketing of democracy itself (Laufer and Paradeise, 1990). This use of SM is distinct from political marketing that is concerned with the promotion of individuals and parties primarily for the purpose of securing electoral support (see for example, Newman, 1994).

THE ASIAN CRISIS, ECONOMIC RESTRUCTURING, SOCIAL MARKETING AND SOCIAL ENGINEERING

In addition to the foregoing, SM is used to promote tangible, measurable outcomes such as lifting productivity, consumer-buying behavior supporting national produce and investor confidence in a national economy. While all three are important to ER, in the wake of the 1997 Asian capital market crisis, the latter-the marketing of place or the nation-has particular significance. While many leading writers have agreed with Ohmae's (1995) contention that the nation-state is becoming redundant in the face of global markets, the Asian crisis has shown that nation-states, while under pressure from globalization, are far from redundant. Nations and regions and cities within nations seek to market themselves as producers, tourist destinations and optimal locations for investment to global markets (Kotler, Haider and Rein, 1993; Kotler, Jutusripitak and Maesincee, 1997; Ward, 1998) in intense competition with other nations, often their regional neighbours.

The Asian crisis has been described as part of a larger crisis of global capitalist competition as Russia and Brazil were also drawn into the market and currency turmoil (Soros, 1998). However, the effects were

most striking in Asia where the economic systems of the "tiger" economies were held up as exemplars of ER by nearly all leading commentators apart from Paul Krugman (1994). Certainly SM techniques were
applied to ER across Asia as the NIC transitional economies faced great
social dislocation of the type seen in developed nations two hundred
years earlier in the Industrial Revolution. Also, internal Asian model-
ling was occurring where the less developed nations such as Vietnam,
China and Indonesia looked to the more developed nations such as Japan, Singapore, the Republic of Korea, Thailand and Malaysia as
guides to SM and ER policy directions (Shultz and Pecotich, 1997).

Some in Asia saw the crisis as a conspiracy by ex-colonialists who
sought not to globalize but to *gobble-ise* Asian market value
(Navaratnam, 1999, pp. 61-62) or as a result of deliberate actions of
cavalier international financiers such as George Soros, who was especially singled out in a variety of fora by Malaysia's Prime Minister
Mahathir Mohamad (see for example, Mahathir, 1998). The crisis origi-
nated in the Thai financial sector in 1997 and spread throughout the region as currency traders sold the overvalued local currencies short
(Soros, 1998, pp. 135-138). This precipitated dramatic devaluations and
a collapse of investment and investor confidence. The role of ER
changed dramatically to counter the crisis and equally SM had to be re-
applied to maintain stability and to reassure national populaces that the
crisis could be contained and the previous path to prosperity regained
(see Mahathir, 1998, for the Malaysian approach).

While Australasia (Australia and New Zealand) was not caught in the
initial turmoil, there has been a gradual in-tandem decline in their currencies' valuations, that by 2001 were significantly lower than their previous regional benchmark of Singapore and also against the basket of
currencies of their major trading partners. The message for governments in all of the regional governments was clear, that the crisis had in-
tensified competition between nation-states to recover their previous
position and growth-rates.

Such competition relates directly to prospects for ER as success depends on marketing of place, nation or region over another or others.
Competition may take obvious, tangible forms such as in the competition between Hong Kong, Kuala Lumpur and Singapore to provide air-
port facilities suitable to establish and/or maintain an air travel regional
hub. Or competition may take less tangible forms of presenting a nation
as a politically and socially stable entity with a recognizable and
friendly "face."

SM, both internally and externally applied, is critical to success in the face of such competition. In the wake of the Asian crisis, both Asian (for example, Navaratnam, 1999) and international (for example, Soros, 1998) commentators have identified national and international investor confidence as being a key to both the conditions creating the crisis and the solutions to it, albeit from very divergent positions in the case of the two writers cited. Successful ER and recovery from the crisis requires the co-ordinated mobilization of national resources that, in turn, relies on SE. For SE to be effective it has to be broadly accepted and "bottom-up" in nature, and SM with the support of PR provides the means to deliver this end.

CONCLUSION

On a global scale, ER is being pursued as a way of adjusting to and anticipating the exigencies of globalized markets and intensifying competition between nation-states. Governments need to mobilize the support of their populations to ensure that ER is effective, but old "top-down" SE models are no longer applicable and have been shown to be manifest failures, especially in pre-1989 Central and Eastern Europe. ER must have the support of the national population and this form of SE must be delivered with broad popular consent through "bottom-up" means, using extensive PR techniques.

SM, by emulating the successes and expectations of private sector commercial marketing, provides a means of meeting the conditions for securing SE outcomes to support ER. While SM is widely deployed and extensively practiced, it has not yet been recognized nor researched as deeply as its importance warrants.

REFERENCES

Andreasen, A. (1995). *Marketing Social Change*. San Francisco: Jossey-Bass.
Bandura, A. (1969). *The Principles of Behavior Modification*. New York: Holt, Rinehart and Winston.
Bartels, R. (1962). *The Development of Marketing Thought*. Homewood, Illinois: Irwin.
Broom, G. and Dozier, D. (1990). *Using Research in Public Relations*. New Jersey: Prentice Hall.
Cuitlip, S., Center, A. and Broom, G. (1985). *Effective Public Relations*. New Jersey: Prentice Hall.

Drucker, P. (1954). *The Practice of Management.* New York: Harper & Row.

Goldberg, M., Fishbein, M. and Middlestadt, S. (1997). *Social Marketing.* Mahwah, New Jersey: Lawrence Erlbaum.

Jenkins, F. (1988). *Public Relations Techniques.* London: Heinemann.

Krugman, P. (1994). The Myth of Asia's Economic Miracle. *Foreign Affairs,* 73(6).

Kotler, P. (1972). *Marketing Management.* New Jersey: Prentice Hall.

Kotler, P. and Levy, S. (1969). Broadening the Marketing Concept. *Journal of Marketing,* (January) Volume 33, pp. 10-15.

Kotler, P. and Roberto, E. (1989). *Social Marketing.* New York: The Free Press.

Kotler, P. and Zaltman, G. (1971). Social Marketing: An Approach to Planned Social Change. *Journal of Marketing,* (July) Volume 35, 3-12.

Kotler, P., Haider, D. and Rein, I. (1993). *Marketing Places.* New York: The Free Press.

Kotler, P., Jutusripitak, S. and Maesincee, S. (1997). *The Marketing of Nations,* New York: The Free Press.

Laufer, R. and Paradeise, C. (1990). *Marketing Democracy.* New Brunswick: Transaction.

Mahathir, M. (1998). *The Challenges of Turmoil.* Selangor Darul Eshan, Malaysia: Pelanduk.

Navaratnam, R. (1999). *Healing the Wounded Tiger.* Selangor Darul Eshan, Malaysia: Pelanduk.

Newman, B. (1994). *The Marketing of the President.* Thousand Oaks, California: Sage.

Ohmae, K. (1995). *The End of the Nation State.* New York: The Free Press.

Peachment, A., Ewing, M.T. and McMahon, L. (1999). Co-branding as a Social Marketing Initiative. *Journal of Contemporary Issues in Business and Government,* 5, 2, 35-40.

Shultz, C. and Pecotich, A. (1997). Marketing and Development in Transition Economies of Southeast Asia: Policy Explication, Assessment and Implications. *Journal of Marketing and Public Policy,* 16(1), 55-68.

Popper, K. (1957). *The Poverty of Historicism.* London: Routledge and Keegan Paul.

Sheth, J. (1974). An investigation of relationships among evaluative beliefs, affect, behavioral intention and behavior. In Farley, J., Ring, H. and Ring, L. *Consumer Behavior, Theory and Application.* Boston: Allyn and Bacon.

Skinner, B. (1948). *Walden Two.* New York: Holt, Rinehart and Winston.

Soros, G. (1998). *The Crisis of Global Capitalism.* London: Little, Brown.

Thorndike, E. (1905). *The Elements of Psychology.* New York: Seiler.

Ward, S. (1998). *Selling Places.* London: Routledge.

Wasik, J. (1996). *Green Marketing & Management: A Global Perspective.* Malden, Massachusetts: Blackwell.

Index